**IMPROVE YOUR CHILDREN'S READING SKILLS
WHILE STRETCHING THEIR MINDS
AND IMAGINATIONS**

For Reading Out Loud!

"A splendidly practical book. . . . You may have been read-ing aloud for years without acquiring this much useful in-formation." —*The Plain Dealer* (Cleveland)

"Invaluable. . . . Two veteran spell-casters annotate 140 child-tested books they highly recommend. Their enthu-siasm for books and strong dedication to the read-aloud cause come across clearly." —*Booklist*

"A top-notch new book for parents and teachers . . . packed with information." —*Sun-Times* (Chicago)

"The authors have gone beyond stock literature for children into promising new areas." —*John Barkham Reviews*

"A wealth of information for parents and teachers on read-ing aloud to children." —*American Bookseller*

For Reading Out Loud!

A GUIDE TO SHARING BOOKS WITH CHILDREN

Margaret Mary Kimmel & Elizabeth Segel

Foreword by Betsy Byars

A DELL TRADE PAPERBACK

A DELL TRADE PAPERBACK

Published by
Dell Publishing Co., Inc.
1 Dag Hammarskjold Plaza
New York, New York 10017

Reprinted by arrangement with Delacorte Press
Printed in the United States of America
First Dell Trade Paperback printing—February 1984

Second printing—March 1984

To our families . . . those who once read to us
and those who have listened

Acknowledgments

This book began in conversations with librarian and educator Elizabeth Fast, whose untimely death in 1977 was a sad loss on many counts. Although both the content and format of the book have changed radically, we wish to acknowledge her important contribution. Other colleagues in Pittsburgh and around the country have helped in many ways, especially Amy Kellman, Marilyn Hollinshead, and Joan Friedberg, who constitute an enviable and much appreciated support system. Students at Simmons College and the University of Pittsburgh, friends, public school officials, teachers, and librarians have generously shared with us their successes and difficulties in reading aloud to children. We are grateful to them all. Thanks are also due to Kathy Foster for her assistance in tracking down books and checking publishing information and to Alyce Patterson for her consistent good work and good cheer.

Contents

Foreword

Most authors enjoy reading their own books aloud and will do so with the slightest encouragement. This is not because we know how the writing should sound and therefore can emphasize the important parts, pause in the right places, and in general do a bang-up job. Indeed, some authors read so nervously that their voices quiver. Others give their own words no more expression than they would give a recipe. The authors who read with a flair and gusto and take the parts of frogs or whales or ten-year-olds with complete, unselfconscious abandon are a glorious rarity.

I think authors like to read aloud because it's a natural part of writing. We read to ourselves as we write, and it is not unusual to read a particular passage six or seven times, changing a phrase here and there with each reading. Perhaps, when we read aloud for others, we are reliving that satisfying moment when we secretly thought, "It's perfect now."

When my children were growing up, they were not eager to listen to me read from my own books, no matter how perfect the passages, so I read them lots of other authors. This was a heady experience. I edited at will, shortened lengthy paragraphs, added dialogue, occasionally punched up a weak ending. Sometimes my changes would be so drastic that the child would cry, "Read it right, Mom, or I'm not going to listen."

I would have felt the same way as a child. I was such an emotional reader. I thought everybody was. I thought all mothers asked their children not to make so many faces when they read and reminded them again and again, "It's just a story."

I know now that this ability to become totally involved in the printed page is a special, life-enriching gift. And those of us—teachers, authors, parents—who take great pleasure in reading both get and give pleasure when we read aloud. I believe this book can help us.

Betsy Byars

Preface

We had both been teaching children's literature at the University of Pittsburgh for several terms—Maggie in the library school and Elizabeth in the English department—before we discovered each other. And a happy discovery it was, for we soon found that in spite of our very different training and experience, we share a common goal. For both of us, all our teaching and writing is ultimately aimed at getting good books to children. And we both are passionately convinced that there's no better way to do this than by reading aloud.

We come by this conviction naturally. Each of us treasures memories of being read to by parents and teachers, and in Maggie's case, by Great-aunt Kate of County Donegal, who was such a spellbinder that "she could have held our attention reading the telephone book." Maggie had carried on the family tradition by reading many a story to children from Baltimore, Boston, and Gary, Indiana, to Aberystwyth, Wales, during her years as a school and public librarian. In those years Elizabeth had a willing audience at home in her two children. She also found herself

occasionally reading aloud passages from Dickens or
Dante, Austen or Angelou, in the literature courses
she taught and discovered that students both enjoyed
and profited from it. In recent years we've both been
blessed with small nieces and nephews who like to
hear books as much as we like to read them.

So it's not surprising that in our classes and in the
frequent workshops we lead for teachers, parents, and
librarians, we urge adults to read to children regularly.
Not many people do these days, we've found. Many
wistfully view it as a feature of "the good old days,"
gone the way of sleigh rides and husking bees. Others
claim that there just aren't enough hours in the day; or
they think they don't read fluently enough; or they
don't know how to pick a book children will like.
Teachers often say that their superiors disapprove,
viewing reading aloud as "entertainment" that takes
time children should spend "working." We've also discovered in these sessions, however, that with our encouragement and suggestions, most adults are willing
—and some eager—to give reading aloud a try.

Now and then a fellow believer stops to share ideas
after a session. *A Toad for Tuesday* kept a second-
grade class enthralled. *Ozma of Oz* made a convert out
of a father who thought he didn't like the Oz books.
Do we know any new animal stories? What would we
recommend for a nine-year-old budding scientist?

Out of such encounters we conceived the idea of
writing a guidebook for these adults—those who already read aloud to children and those who, with a
little help, are willing to try. A resource that will

- point out the specific benefits of reading aloud to school-aged children;
- suggest ways of finding or making time to read aloud, at home and in the classroom;
- and finally, list and describe a variety of outstanding books that are good choices for reading aloud to children from kindergarten age through eighth grade —140 titles in all.

For Maggie, the project had special meaning, for it was the revival of an idea she and her colleague Elizabeth Fast had talked about years ago. Long hours of discussion, discovery, writing and rewriting followed as the book slowly took shape. The biggest job was deciding on those 140 books. Our tastes are different, and countless hours were spent just talking about particular books. No matter how long it took, we arrived at a consensus before any book was included or rejected.

When the list was complete, our uneasy awareness that we had no doubt missed some worthy titles was balanced by the excitement of being able to share with readers so many books that we admire—books that had entertained and enriched us both.

A Word About the Scope of This Guide

The guide focuses on children of elementary and middle school age because many parents and professionals already recognize the importance of reading aloud to preschoolers but don't always understand the value of reading aloud to older children. Moreover,

excellent guides to sharing books with children in the
early years are already available: *Babies Need Books*,
by Dorothy Butler (Atheneum, 1981), and *Choosing
Books for Children*, by Betsy Hearne (Delacorte,
1981), are particularly helpful. And while high school
students can certainly enjoy and profit from hearing
books read aloud, by high school age the possibilities
of *what* to read have expanded to include the whole
of literature. In addition, adults generally know more
about good reading-aloud material from "adult" writers like Poe and Dickens and Conan Doyle than they
do about the outstanding literature that has been written for children.

Two other decisions need to be explained. Picture
books are and should be staples of any reading-aloud
program for five- and six-year-olds, and the increasing
number of more sophisticated picture books being published should also be shared with older children. Yet
we have not included picture books in our list of
recommended books. This is in part because the true
picture book relies on the illustrations to help tell the
story and our central aim is to provide the experiences
of *listening* to literature. Besides, adults can skim a
picture book and decide for themselves whether it
would be a good choice more easily than they can
with a longer book.

Finally, although no program of reading aloud would
be complete without poetry, adding books of poetry to
our list would have doubled the size of this volume.
So we have merely included a short list of our personal
favorites among the many fine poetry collections avail-

able, with brief suggestions on choosing poems for children of different ages and on reading them aloud (Appendix A).

Margaret Mary Kimmel
Elizabeth Segel

I/Why Bother?

THE VALUE OF READING ALOUD

> *"I remember little from my childhood, but the soft voice reading to me still lingers inside my mind."*

How vividly most people remember the experience of being read to as children! They can tell you exactly whether it was mother or dad who read at bedtime. They know it was Aunt Lou who specialized in Kipling, and Mrs. Rossi in third grade who read *Charlotte's Web* the last thing every afternoon.

A loved adult's voice conjuring up a colorful story-world . . . the memory evokes such warm and contented feelings as recollections of infant nursing might hold, if we could remember back that far. Indeed, the two experiences have common elements: the physical and emotional closeness of adult and child, the adult's attentiveness to the child, and the aim of satisfying a hunger. Clearly, both activities are nurturing ones.

A middle-aged woman recalls "a sweet, familiar voice" reading at bedtime. "I remember little from my childhood," she says, "but the soft voice reading to me still lingers inside my mind."

Augusta Baker, now retired from her long service as Coordinator of Children's Services for the New York Public Library, confesses that she, too, has few memories from her primary school years. "I don't remember the teachers who poured the information in my head, who taught the basic skills . . . [though] they were important. My vivid memory is that of a teacher— probably fourth grade—who read a chapter every week of *Beautiful Joe*, a story which was the 'Perils of Pauline' of the canine world." She feels she owes her love of books and reading in large part to that teacher.

A colleague's face brightens when the subject of children's books comes up in party conversation. "You know," he confides, "when I was a boy, I went to a camp where, along with the usual games and sports, the owner read to us every day after lunch. Boys lay sprawled about everywhere while from the dining-hall steps this small white-haired lady read another install- ment of *Tom Sawyer* or whatever the current novel happened to be." The small white-haired lady was Laura Richards, best known as an accomplished writer of humorous verse for children; the poets Ogden Nash and David McCord were among the sprawling boys who benefited from the Camp Merryweather tradition of reading aloud.

As another, younger poet, Karla Kuskin, says: "Those were the days when a channel was simply a deep waterway, sesame was only a seed and people read aloud for entertainment" (*The New York Times Book Review*, November 15, 1981, p. 57). Such entertain- ment wasn't just for children, either; whole families often gathered in the evening and someone read from a classic novel or the latest magazine serial while the others worked—sewed or hooked a rug, mended tools or shelled nuts.

Nor were communal reading sessions limited to the home and family. Studs Terkel, for his book *American*

Dreams (Pantheon Books, 1980), interviewed ninety-four-year-old Dora Rosenzweig, who immigrated to Chicago as a child from a Jewish ghetto in Russia. At twelve, having completed sixth grade, she took a job as a cigar maker, where she worked in a room of thirty to forty people. She recalls: "They elected me a reader. I used to roll fifty cigars an hour. That was my piece-work limit. So if I read for an hour, they would donate the fifty cigars I missed. If I read for two hours, they'd give me a hundred . . . I would choose the books. Whoever heard of a twelve-year-old girl reading Flaubert's *Salammbô*? Whatever struck me, I'd read to the others. Tolstoi, anything" (Terkel, p. 108).

But is the disappearance of communal reading something to mourn? Perhaps it's just a case of having replaced one pleasant pastime with others—gathering around the television set for *Monday Night Football,* for instance. After all, if today's children were born too late for group reading sessions, Dora Rosenzweig was born too early to have known the satisfaction of racking up a high score on the space-combat video game. Maybe it balances out.

But no. We all recognize that the loss is a real loss, not just a change, and that the shared pleasure of reading aloud is not the only casualty. Many children today grow up with negative attitudes toward books and reading in any form. The media call it "a literacy crisis." The schools try new methods of teaching reading and test children more often, but nothing seems to cure the problem. Publishers bring out attractive books geared to poor readers; teachers report that these students are so turned off by books that the new formats don't entice them at all. Worried parents invest in expensive "teach your child to read" kits and high-powered electronic learning games, only to see their children growing up reading nothing on their own but an occasional comic book.

Meanwhile, research data have slowly been accumulating that suggest how we might resolve this crisis. Several studies of children from widely varied backgrounds who learned to read easily and remained good readers throughout their school years have revealed that they had something in common. They all had been read to regularly from early childhood and had as models adults or older children who read for pleasure.

In fact, reading aloud to children from literature that is meaningful to them is now widely acknowledged among experts to be the most effective, as well as the simplest and least expensive, way to foster in children a lifelong love of books and reading. The task now is to pass this word along to individual parents, school administrators, and classroom teachers.

Many of these adults understand the importance of reading aloud to a young child who can't yet read. But too often these same adults no more think of reading aloud to the child who has learned to read than they would continue to run alongside the child's first bicycle, steadying the vehicle, after the child had learned to ride alone.

This is a sad mistake. READING ALOUD SHOULD CONTINUE ALL THROUGH THE SCHOOL YEARS, for many reasons.

- *To stop the read-aloud sessions of the preschool years ends a rich shared experience.* A mother and father we know were concerned because their son's first-grade year was nearly over and he showed no signs of being able to read. They expressed their concern to his teacher and asked if she thought he needed special help to overcome a problem or disability. She stared at them in surprise: "Why, Jason reads quite well—and has been for several months now." It turned out that Jason had been keeping his new skill a secret, worrying that if his parents knew he could read to himself, they might stop reading him a bedtime story. Needless to say, Jason's parents reassured him that he could enjoy reading to himself *and* have his nightly story, too.

In many families now grown up, books read aloud together in childhood have become a treasured part of family history. "Remember when you read us *Five Children and It,* and we kids spent our entire week at the beach digging for a sand-fairy?" "I'll never forget when Mom was reading *Cheaper by the Dozen* in the car and Dad got laughing so hard that he had to pull over and stop."

In school, too, the shared experience that reading aloud provides creates a genuine bond in a group of diverse children that is unlikely to occur in any other way. As one teacher said after reading *A Bridge to Terabithia* to her class: "By the end of that story, we had been through so much together."

And this kind of communal experience is becoming rarer. In automobile assembly plants these days, many workers are plugged into their individual "walkaround" tape players. No doubt these help dispel the tedium of the job, but such gadgets cut off one worker from another; each is operating in his or her own world rather than sharing, as the cigar workers did, one fictional world.

• *Being read to promotes, rather than retards, children's desire to read independently.* Contrary to some parents' and teachers' fears, listening to stories doesn't make "lazy readers." Rather, what the children hear seems to whet their appetites to read that book or others like it for themselves. One school librarian told us that when she asks children to name their favorite book, they almost always name the book she or their teacher has most recently read to them.

We all know that film and television adaptations increase interest in a book. When *The Secret Garden* was telecast on *Once Upon a Classic*, copies of the book were scarce as hen's teeth in the libraries. (We know one little girl whose popularity shot up considerably as her classmates competed to borrow the copy she owned.) Reading a story aloud is another form of book promotion and is just as effective with the children it reaches as a *Star Wars* movie or an *Afterschool Special* on television. And it has the decided advantage that the individual parent or professional—not Madison Avenue or Hollywood—can choose what book to promote to a particular child or group of children.

One reason that reading a book or story works so

effectively to motivate independent reading is that learning to read is difficult and often frustrating. Going on to read more and more challenging books means repeatedly risking failure. Hearing a first-rate story read aloud makes the rewards of sticking to it clear and tangible.

- *Being read to fosters improvement of children's independent reading skills.* Studies of first- and second-graders and fourth- through sixth-graders have demonstrated that children who are read aloud to on a regular basis over a period of several months show significant gains in reading comprehension, decoding skills, and vocabulary. (See the McCormick article cited in Appendix B for a summary of these studies.) The gains were greatest for disadvantaged students but not limited to them—all the children benefited significantly compared to the control groups, who were read to only occasionally or not at all.

  Besides making children more eager to tackle the difficult tasks involved in learning to read, hearing stories read gets children used to the written language they will meet in books, which is different from spoken language.

- *All through their school years, young people can enjoy listening to books that would be too difficult for them to read on their own.* How exciting it is for the first-grader, who is struggling to read brief and perhaps insipid primer stories, to share the delights and dangers of a whole prairie year when the teacher reads a daily chapter from one of Laura Ingalls

Wilder's books. Similarly, seventh-graders might find *The Wizard of Earthsea* beyond their ability or ambition for independent reading yet become totally absorbed in listening to an adult read it aloud.

Listening experiences like these are especially valuable for the student whose home language is not English and for children whose chief exposure to English comes from the television set.

- *Wonderful books that are "hard to get into" are more accessible when read aloud.* The first few pages of an unfamiliar book usually determine whether a child reading independently will go on or give up and look for another book. In some books the reader immediately knows what's going on and is almost instantly swept up in the events of the story. Fairy tales, for example, signal in the first few sentences who the characters are, whether they are good or bad, and what their predicament is. A formula story of a less exalted sort, like a Nancy Drew mystery or a Spiderman comic, also makes the reader feel right at home in familiar territory. But some of the richest, most rewarding books are the unconventional ones, the ones that don't fit a formula. Such books may defer gratification of the reader's curiosity in order to first establish a scene and mood; they are original rather than predictable. These books profit immensely from being read aloud. Your captive audience may be a bit restless until they get oriented, but they will soon be deep in the world of story with you if you have selected well.

- *For the poor student whose inability to read has barred her or him from access to stimulating material in every subject, including literature, there is no substitute for reading aloud.* The attempt of publishers to be responsive to the needs of poor readers by providing high-interest/low-level-of-difficulty books is praiseworthy, but the fact is that many literary experiences that would be moving and meaningful to a fifteen-year-old reading at a third-grade level simply cannot be conveyed in simple sentence structure and vocabulary. Reading aloud is a way to be sure these students aren't deprived of their rich literary heritage.

- *A significant number of children will always grasp material better through their ears than through their eyes.* When asked in a class, one student said he had no early memory of books. He didn't remember ever enjoying a book and doesn't read anything now except required assignments—not even the newspaper. He did recall with pleasure, however, records of stories that he owned as a child—folktales, Hans Christian Andersen stories, and the like. "Words on the page somehow come between me and the story" is the way he described his problem. He was envious of his classmates' memories of their parents reading to them. He was sure that would have been even better than the records.

  There are others like this young man who may never find pleasure in reading, even if they have been read to in childhood. Is reading to such youngsters a waste of time, then? Not at all. Ideally, they should have occasional opportunities to listen to literature all their lives, so that they, too, can savor the unique pleasures of the written word.

• *Studies have shown that reading aloud to children significantly broadens their reading interests and tastes.* Children and adolescents who tend to limit themselves to one author's books or one type of book in their independent reading—mysteries or sports stories or romances, for instance—will often be led to more challenging books and greater variety in their reading by hearing a book chosen by a knowledgeable adult.

• *Exposing children to good literature, presented for enjoyment, will increase the chances that their reading life doesn't end with high school graduation.* A major goal of the schools should be to turn out people who not only are able to read but find enough pleasure in reading that they will actually read a book now and then after they've left school. We know that many American adults simply never read books; of these, only a small number are actually unable to read. In all likelihood, the adults who can but do not read books were once students who read only what was required of them at school. Once the assignments stopped, so did the reading. A few good books read aloud solely for the students' enjoyment could have made a difference.

• *Seeing adults reading with enjoyment increases the chances that children will become lifelong readers.*

This means that the parent, teacher, librarian, grand-parent, or other adult who finds time to read to a child and does it with enthusiasm is providing a model as well as a story. Observing adults who are eager to read and are engaged in reading is more effective in making readers of children than any number of lectures on the importance of reading.

And it's important to recognize that, though the parent makes a very effective model, children whose parents have never discovered the pleasures of reading need not be left out. Any adult or older child can fill this role. By providing regular reading-aloud sessions to children who do not get that experience at home, the school or day-care center or library can break through the cycle of illiteracy that victimizes many young people. Then when these children who have enjoyed hearing stories grow up, they may very well pass on the pleasure by reading to the children in their lives.

II/Fitting It In:

FINDING OR MAKING TIME TO READ ALOUD

> *"I don't have time to listen to stories."*
> *"Are you kidding? Only babies get read to."*
> *"What about my TV shows?"*

In the Home . . .

From time to time we all run across a nostalgic description of family reading sessions in bygone years—cheerful, cozy scenes painted by adults looking back on their happy childhood days. One of the most vivid occurs in "Recipe for a Magic Childhood," written some years ago by the distinguished novelist and educator Mary Ellen Chase for the *Ladies' Home Journal.* She described the kitchen in which the winters of her Maine childhood were spent—warm black wood stove, red and white checked tablecloth, red geraniums at the window, and her young mother cooking and baking, washing and ironing while the four children played or read nearby (school didn't meet during January and February in Maine). "My mother usually somehow managed, at eleven, to sit down for half an hour in the red rocking chair by the window," she related.

> She called this half hour her "respite," a word which early charmed me; and . . . she would allow us to sit upon our red stools while . . . she herself would read aloud to us. Here was the very doorsill

to complete enchantment, for she was seemingly
as lost as we in whatever she was reading. The
iron teakettle simmered . . . , the red geraniums
glowed with life; smells of our approaching dinner
filled our noses from stewpans or baking dishes;
while my mother's voice brought trooping into our
kitchen all those with whom we rejoiced or suffered, admired or feared, loved or hated.

> (Reprinted in Phyllis Fenner,
> *Something Shared: Children and Books*
> [New York: John Day Co., 1959],
> pp. 15–16)

Who can read that without a moment's pang of
envy, followed by an impulsive resolution to provide
such "a magic childhood" for the children in our lives,
too. Then the chilly breath of reality reminds the
mothers among us that they don't spend the entire
day in the kitchen (thank heaven). Whether their
daily work is pursued in the home or outside it, they
do not spend long hours every day with their school-
aged children, as Mary Ellen Chase's mother did. And
for both parents, the time when the family is all together at home is likely to be when the parents are
tired and needing a bit of time to themselves.

Yet today's parents can learn from this woman.
Notice that she called the reading-aloud ritual her
"respite." She, too, was tired from all that cooking on
the wood stove and laundering without benefit of
automatic washer and dryer. Her use of the term
"respite" suggests that reading to her children was for
her a valid excuse for letting the housework wait. And

it still is—just as valid for the factory-worker or bank-executive parent who returns from a full day's work to a messy house as it was for the Maine housewife decades ago. "Respite" also implies rest, and reading aloud does take less of a weary parent's energy than refereeing the arguments of cranky children or listening to the shrieks and racing around of overexcited ones.

But, you may be thinking, there are still the kids to persuade. And you're right. After the preschool years, one of the major obstacles to regular reading aloud in families is the children's own resistance. You should be prepared to encounter these reactions:

- Suzy (twelve years old, good reader): "But I baby-sit on weekends and school nights I have to do my homework, and practice the piano, and — oh, yes — wash my hair. I don't have time to listen to stories."
- Joe (a ten-year-old who never picks up a book voluntarily and suffers agonies over reading assignment): "Are you kidding? Only babies get read to."
- Mary Ann (eight years old; she loved being read to until recently): "What about my TV shows? I have to watch *Little House on the Prairie* and the reruns of *Happy Days* and . . . and . . . and . . ."

Let's start with the last problem. *To make time for reading aloud in the home, you are going to have to take a stand against unlimited television viewing.* Some would argue that television can take the place of reading; print will soon be obsolete, they say. Children can get lots of stories just by flipping on the TV —why fight it?

The differences between reading and watching television are many and complicated, and numerous books and articles have been written to explore them (see, for example, the Winn and Singer entries in the Bibliography, Appendix B). For our purposes, a few brief points will suffice:

- Television watching is less personal and more passive than listening to a family member read a story. When listening to someone reading, a child automatically creates mental pictures of the scenes and actions described. With television, nothing is left to the visual imagination. In addition, the television narrative cannot be stopped for questions or discussions and started again (at least, with the equipment in most homes). Thus it gives children no practice in using language.

- Television segments are often so short that children who watch a great deal are unable to sustain their interest and stick to an activity for more than a few minutes. Teachers complain that schoolchildren today have short attention spans long after they should have outgrown them. Read-aloud sessions, short for young children and extended (usually by popular demand) as they grow older, can remedy this problem.

- Watching television is not a shared experience in most families; reading aloud is. Even when children's viewing time is limited, they probably do much of their watching when the parent is busy— fixing dinner, for instance—and not present. Using *Sesame Street* for a baby-sitter while you get the meal on the table doesn't make you a negligent parent, but we all know about the powerful temptation to leave the kids in front of the set while you pay bills, talk on the phone, catch up on work, take a bath, or watch *your* favorite program on the second TV set. We have to resist that temptation. And there's no time to lose: experts estimate that children of elementary-school age average four and one half to five hours of television watching a day (see Singer article referred to in Appendix B). That doesn't leave time for much reading of any sort!

Although it's hard to change established household patterns, it can be done . . . even when the issue is limiting television viewing. When local teachers went on strike, a woman we know foresaw that her children would begin watching television around the clock. So on the first day of the strike she announced to her seven- and nine-year-olds that they would be limited to two hours of television a day—one hour in the daytime and one in the evening. She then braced herself, expecting howls of outrage. Instead, her children dashed off to find the newspaper so that they could decide what programs would make up their quota for that day. Could it be that children would welcome more leadership in such matters than we think?

As for son Joe's reaction to the prospect of family reading sessions, if you never *stop* reading to your children, you may avoid the charge of babyishness. Otherwise, we recommend asking Joe to give you a trial period. Then choose that first book *very* carefully with Joe's interests in mind. (The listing of surefire books in Chapter V is a good starting point.)

It's especially important to break down the resistance of a child like Joe to being read to, precisely because of his difficulties as an independent reader. Having a parent sit down with him and read aloud the first chapter of a dreaded assigned novel can give a considerable boost to Joe's understanding and enjoyment of the book. And if his parents show him that reading aloud and listening are pleasurable for adults as well as small children, half the battle is won.

With children as old as Suzy—junior high and high

school age—increasing activities outside the home may make frequent reading sessions difficult. We know one family with teen-agers, though, who managed family reading nearly every day. One person read aloud while the others did the dinner dishes (shades of the cigar makers!). If something like this won't work, perhaps you could manage a regular session once a week—Sunday evening might be a good time.

Don't give up on the idea, however, if you can't manage a regular time. Watch for those serendipitous moments. The reading aloud of an appropriate story can become a family tradition at holiday celebrations. This, of course, is already a ritual for many—the Gospel story of Jesus' birth on Christmas Eve; reading the story of Queen Esther and wicked Haman on Purim. Many wonderful secular stories exist as well that the whole family will enjoy: *Mister Corbett's Ghost*, for example, on New Year's Eve, *Zlateh the Goat* during Hanukkah, a favorite ghost story to spook Halloween guests.

Take along a book when you anticipate a long wait somewhere—the dentist's or doctor's office, for instance. You'll probably attract other children as you read, earning the gratitude of their parents as a bonus.

Another occasion for reading aloud arises when a child is too sick to go out but well enough to enjoy a story. Elizabeth remembers her bout with measles at ten: "I itched and had horrible feverish nightmares that I still remember, but the worst part was that the shades were drawn and I wasn't allowed to read. One of my fondest memories of my father is of him reading to me then. Even at the time I appreciated what a labor of love it must have been, for he read all the way through a book that was my favorite but probably would not have been his choice—*Little Women*."

Sometimes family vacations are a perfect time for reading aloud. With no television (if you're lucky), no homework, and no job demands, it's not difficult to find time for reading. If you're traveling, try to choose a book that is related to the area you're visiting. Take along a sea story if you're heading for the shore, or a historical novel that will make a stop at a national landmark more meaningful. One year the Segel family read *Across Five Aprils* driving to Gettysburg and back. This story of the Civil War as experienced by a young farmboy in southern Illinois brought to life the events of the distant past, peopling the quiet, grassy vistas with ghostly men and boys who had been, the family realized, the children and brothers and fathers of others suffering all across the country. Our list of book-places in Chapter VI is designed to help you coordinate reading choices with a travel itinerary.

If you can read in the car (the trick is to shield your eyes so you don't see the countryside whizzing by), you'll find that reading aloud makes the time pass more quickly for children—and for the driver, too.

A graduate student we know pointed out that the pleasures of vacation reading need not be limited to families with children. When she and her husband were vacationing together, she heard him chuckling over a book. "What's so funny?" she asked. That was the beginning of four summers of seashore vacations with Mark Twain. And when a friend of ours became ill on her honeymoon, it prompted her husband to devote himself to reading Sherlock Holmes stories to her—something they both remember fondly.

Finally, parents who are away from home and their children a good deal can maximize the benefit of the time they can devote to reading aloud by taping each reading session on a portable tape recorder (it need not be a fancy one for adequate voice reproduction). The child who has access to a simple tape player can then hear a mother's or dad's voice reading the story again and again while the parent is at work or on a trip. Quite a library of taped literature can be built up this way, and when the children of a family outgrow particular stories, they can be passed on to friends. Listening to a tape is no substitute, of course, for actual reading sessions with their sharing and cuddling, so be sure to continue with "live" reading sessions whenever possible.

In the Schools . . .

> *Literature itself is a survival tool, "equipment for living," as Kenneth Burke says. It must not be elbowed aside.*

Despite all the research evidence and expert opinion as to the value of reading aloud to children, precious little of it seems to be going on in the schools. Most children we talk to report that, after kindergarten, only one or two teachers read aloud to them with any regularity. Why aren't more teachers using this simple, inexpensive, and effective educational practice?

For one thing, although the current movement for accountability by the schools has its good points, it discourages teachers from reading to their students. Accountability rests on testing and test results. When a school's success is judged by its students' performances on standardized tests, testable skills take priority in teaching; teachers understandably "teach to the tests" and are expected to do so. Tests, unfortunately, are limited in what they can measure. A student's warm memory of a story shared with classmates and teacher can't be quantified on a test, even if that memory will last sixty years. A test won't indicate which children will turn to books for pleasure and for continued learning in the years after graduation and which ones will never open a book from one year of their adult lives to the next.

The increasing emphasis on learning programs— such as sets of materials, audiovisual sequences, or computer-based learning programs—also reduces the opportunities for reading to children in the classroom. Once the school system has bought expensive kits, workbooks, dittoes, and videotapes, they must be used, and little time is left for activities developed by the teacher. A great advantage of reading aloud is that one teacher or aide and one book can provide thirty or forty children at once with a rich learning experience. This alone should recommend it in these cost-conscious times. But the very fact that it costs nothing for a teacher to read aloud from a library book entails a serious handicap as well—namely, that there are no salesmen or advertising budgets devoted to convincing educators of the virtues of this activity.

Another serious consequence of these skill-based learning programs is that they separate the process of learning to read from the child's experience of the value of reading. As Frank Smith has pointed out: "All programs fractionate learning experience. . . . With their inevitably limited objectives, programs teach trivial aspects of literacy and they can teach that literacy is trivial" ("Demonstrations, Engagement and Sensitivity: The Choice Between People and Programs," *Language Arts* [September 1981], 637, 640). At the very least, learning programs should be supplemented by the experience of hearing first-rate literature read aloud, giving children a better reason for learning to read than to pass a test.

The "Back to Basics" mood that has characterized public opinion in recent years also has not been conducive to reading aloud in the schools. This is surprising, since reading aloud was a standard feature of the traditional classroom that proponents of this approach look to as a touchstone. Besides, reading aloud is surely one of the most basic of educational practices. The explanation seems to be that this view of education stems in part from a dismay at what was considered an overemphasis on the child's enjoyment of learning, i.e., "learning through play." There was some truth to the criticism that the less appealing but necessary hard work of learning was neglected in some schools—the memorization needed to master English grammar or acquire a working vocabulary in a foreign language, for instance. Unfortunately, this criticism was generalized to a suspicion of any classroom activity that smacked of "fun." The very fact that children enjoy being read to works against its acceptance by Back to Basics enthusiasts.

In the face of all this, what can individual teachers do? First, they can tactfully challenge the assumption that enjoyment and learning are mutually exclusive. Using the material in this book and the bibliography, they can spread the word that tests themselves confirm the important educational benefits of reading aloud. Above all, they can resolve to supplement their required materials with frequent reading sessions.

We know it isn't easy to find the time in a hectic school day. Time and again teachers tell us that they'd like to read to their students, but the curriculum allows no time for it. The state or school district mandates so many hours and minutes a day for this subject and that. The middle schools in one district, we are told, are committed to "survival skills"; time that once was available for reading is now assigned to vocational/technical education. This may well be useful, but we believe that literature itself is a survival tool, "equipment for living," as Kenneth Burke says. It must not be elbowed aside.

Each teacher knows the time that might best be set aside in her or his classroom for reading aloud. A regular time is preferable, of course: after lunch to settle children down? twice a week in language arts or reading periods? first thing in the morning with the "homeroom" group? or that traditional slot, the last few minutes of the school day? The possibilities are limited only by your ingenuity.

Teachers who want to promote reading aloud might meet as a group with the school librarian to brainstorm schoolwide plans. On inclement days when children can't go out at lunchtime, a reading-aloud session might be held in the library for those children who wished to come (no compulsory attendance). For older children it might be called a "fantasy club" or "mystery club" and books be chosen accordingly. If your school, like some we know, devotes the afternoon before a holiday to showing mediocre films ("because the kids are too wound up to work"), you might suggest that, instead, pairs of teachers take turns reading to their combined classes. That way teachers' "housekeeping" chores get done and students have a worthwhile experience, too. (Just be sure to pick an exciting story that will grab the attention of those "wound-up" children.)

Be ready, too, for the unexpected bit of time. If you always have a collection of good stories at hand, the bus breakdown that dumps thirty-five rowdy kids on you after a long day won't be a total disaster.

Teachers can extend their effectiveness by encouraging parents to read aloud at home. Polls and studies indicate that the great majority of parents want to help their children become good readers. You can give them guidance in how to do this. Stress the benefits of reading to children at a parent conference or in a letter home, and let parents know what books you will be reading to their child's class. Then suggest other suitable titles at your library for reading to the child at home. Occasionally read the first book in a series in class and let parents and children know that the story continues, suggesting that they get the sequel for home reading (see the list of books with sequels in Chapter V).

Suggest to administrators and parent-teacher organizations that they schedule a parent and staff workshop on reading aloud to children.

If a school newsletter goes home with students, offer to contribute a brief review of a book or two for family reading. And if your school draws up a list of suggested or required summer reading for pupils, indicate books families might share through reading aloud.

Ideally, parents and teachers can join forces to introduce the child to all the varieties of book pleasure. Yet many parents aren't comfortable with books or teachers and may not be receptive to your efforts. If this happens, don't be discouraged. For the child whose parents have never been turned on to reading, it takes just one committed teacher to transform books from symbols of frustration to cherished objects. We realize that such a commitment adds to the burdens of a demanding job, but look at it this way: How else can you make as great an impact on a student's life and mind as through a year's worth of books, selected with intelligence and shared with infectious enthusiasm?

III/Casting a Spell:

HOW TO READ ALOUD EFFECTIVELY

You will be well rewarded for polishing your skills—by the clamor for "just one more" or the nearly silent sigh of satisfaction.

Essentially these suggestions on how to read aloud are directed to readers outside the home, because family members and guests need not be skilled readers to hold even the most restless listener spellbound. Keeping the attention of a group of children is more of a challenge, however. We offer here a few tips that will help the more reluctant or inexperienced reader to gain confidence and the veteran reader to perfect his or her technique.

A word about the audience. Reading aloud, although not a theatrical experience, is a performance. The reader must be aware of audience reaction; of creating a mood that allows the listener to respond to the story. This interaction between reader and listener, between story and audience, is a key to success. This doesn't mean that one needs a stage, or even a fireplace and deep leather chair, but it does mean that the reader has to pay attention to the atmosphere and physical setting of the session as well as the interpretation of the story. Too much heat or polar cold may distract listeners. With a little thought about which corner of the room to use, a quiet place can be created in a busy classroom or library. One librarian found that merely seating a group with their backs to the main activity of the room helped enormously with the problem of distraction. One teacher sat in front of a window that looked out on a pleasant hill but found that the class, facing the bright light, was restless and uncomfortable. The wiggling decreased when she merely switched her chair around and sat the group at an angle from the window.

Make sure that listeners can hear you. Volume control is often difficult for a beginner to regulate, but a simple question like "Can everyone hear me?" does much to reassure fidgety listeners. Since reading out loud is a shared experience, one must look at the audience now and then. Besides confirming the bond between reader and listener, this helps to gauge audience response and thwart rebellion in the back of the room.

Sometimes an epidemic of wiggling is your clue that you have reached the end of children's attention spans, the point at which they cannot keep still, no matter how much they like the story. When this happens, it's best to break off (without scolding) at the next lull in the action, saving the rest for another time. If you are within a page or two of the chapter's end, however, you might just let your audience know that the story is almost over. This often helps the wigglers muster a bit more patience. Then plan to cover less material in subsequent sessions. Some groups of inexperienced listeners may need to begin with sessions as short as ten minutes. In general, however, fifteen to twenty minutes is a reasonable length for reading to primary school groups, thirty minutes about right for middle-graders.

Some children of five, six, and seven can't sit still for anything. Don't assume that such children aren't enjoying being read to. If you can let these active ones sprawl on the floor and move around (something that is admittedly more feasible at home than in school groups), you will probably find that they never wander out of earshot and are, in fact, taking it all in. In many cases they are enjoying the story as much as the child who sits motionless and clearly enthralled.

When you finish reading, don't break the spell by asking trivial questions ("What was the pig's name who won first prize at the county fair?" or "How long was Abel stranded on the island?"). Children get plenty of reading for information in their school careers. For the greatest benefit, most reading aloud should not be associated with testing of any sort; its goal should be simple pleasure.

If children have been moved by a story, they often do not want to discuss it at all right away. Later they may be happy to talk about it—or sing or dance or paint something that expresses how they feel about the story. The important word is "feel." Young children are not equipped to analyze literature. To press for such a response can reduce a complex and deeply felt experience to a chore.

Purists may be shocked, but we have been known to skip sentences, paragraphs, even an occasional chapter, that we judged would lose us the children's attention. Sometimes this means simply omitting a few nonessential phrases in order to reach the end of a chapter before a restless six-year-old's attention span expires. Or one may find that an author has indulged in digressions that spin out too long a book that otherwise has great appeal for children. Even adults who read *Watership Down* silently may find themselves skipping over some of the discursive essays that begin certain chapters, and we recommend doing so when reading the book to children (unless you have very philosophical listeners and all the time in the world).

Occasionally you may want to omit a whole chapter that you judge dull or offensive. This kind of omission can be made only if the narrative is episodic with one adventure following another but not depending on it for plot development. Such omissions of paragraphs or chapters must be carefully planned, so skim the material in advance and mark what you want to skip. You don't want to discover later that you've left out a piece of information that's essential to understanding the book's conclusion.

We have suggested a few such omissions of nonessential material in our annotations of the recommended titles. Most children are bored, we have found, by "The Lobster Quadrille" chapter of *Alice in Wonderland*, with its several long parodies of poems unfamiliar to children today, and by the inane recitations in chapter twenty-one of *The Adventures of Tom Sawyer*.

This kind of editing has a long and distinguished history from the days when oral storytellers, passing on the old tales, left out what didn't please their audiences and elaborated on what did. It should be spar-

ingly used but is a legitimate expression of a good reader's sensitivity to the needs of her or his audience.

Many of the books we recommend have illustrations that you will want to share with your listeners. Nevertheless, we suggest that you wait to show the illustrations until you have read aloud at least part of the book. (Of course, this won't be possible when you are reading to one or two listeners who are sitting right next to you.) We make this suggestion because children in this age of television have many fewer opportunities to form their own mental images than earlier generations did. Experts feel that this impoverishment of the visual imagination is one of the most serious penalties of television viewing. By oral reading, we can provide children with the chance to create their own stormy seas or king's palace. They can collaborate with Stevenson in imagining the terrifying blind pirate Pew and the ingratiating yet treacherous Long John Silver. N. C. Wyeth's illustrations for *Treasure Island* are classics, loved by generations of readers, but they are Wyeth's images, his interpretations. Children can enjoy them all the more if they have first developed their own vivid mental pictures with which to compare them.

Children will probably object to this strategy. Their experience with picture books as well as with television has persuaded them that they can't follow the story if they can't see the pictures. But the illustrated book—unlike the picture book—is not dependent on the picture for meaning, and children can be led to understand this. If you don't train them, you'll find yourself having to interrupt your reading frequently to hold the book up for inspection. And nothing breaks the spell of a story faster than impatient squirms and cries of "I can't see," "Hey, teacher, I can't see!"

How dramatic should your reading be? Some readers are very straightforward. Others sway with the blowing wind and gasp in awe as the heroine saves the day. One bit of advice—keep it simple. Sometimes one is tempted to change the quality or pitch of the voice with different characters. In a short book with one or two characters, this isn't too difficult, but in a book like *Queenie Peavy* it would be a mistake to attempt voice characterizations for the many people Queenie encounters. Even the most experienced reader can mistake one character's tone for another when the reading involves several sessions. Furthermore, such voice characterization often complicates the listening process. On the other hand, one does not want listeners to fall asleep—at least, not usually. A soothing, almost monotonous tone that would be fine at bedtime may lose an audience in the middle of the day.

Whether or not the reading is a dramatic rendition is partly a matter of taste and experience. A more experienced reader can sense when a moment demands a grand gesture or a bellow of rage and perform accordingly. Do be careful with such actions, however. Just such a "bellow" once brought both the principal and the school nurse to the library on the run, and an exuberant father we know knocked a bowl of buttered popcorn sky-high with a sweeping gesture. Dramatization should sound spontaneous, but needs to be carefully planned, especially by beginners. In the annotations for each book, we have tried not only to indicate possible difficulties for the reader, but sometimes to suggest occasions where one might wax eloquent.

Gauging the proper pace of a story is another essential ingredient. If the reading is too slow, the listeners may lose track of the action and become fidgety. "Get on with it, Dad" was one family's complaint. Too fast has some of the same problems—the listener simply can't keep up, can't savor the story. While the reader has some control of the overall pace, there are often parts of the narrative that have an internal rhythm of their own. For instance, Lucinda's pell-mell flight to find Policeman McGonegal and save Tony Coppino's fruit stand from bullies in *Roller Skates* is a breathless race, and Ruth Sawyer built that breathlessness into her phrases and sentences. In *Tuck Everlasting*, Mae Tuck's violent confrontation with the man who is after the water of immortality is a dramatic scene that moves as swiftly as the blink of an eye. The pace of life in the humid, hot days suddenly quickens for both reader and listener. The beginning of *The Iron Giant*, on the other hand, unfolds at a slow and dignified— even portentous—pace, dictated by Ted Hughes's careful choice of word and syntax. Many of our recommended books were chosen in part because the accomplished writers have such control of their material that the reader can't go wrong.

Yet it is through your voice that the author's words reach the listeners. Its tone and pitch color the experience. Music teachers coach their voice students to breathe from the diaphragm, and this admonition certainly applies to those who read aloud—whether just beginning or with hours of experience. Good breathing technique gives substance to a voice that otherwise may be light or high-pitched. It supports the voice and builds the listeners' confidence that you know what you're doing. A breathless quality may be all right when you're reading about the Elephant's Child, breathless with curiosity, as he approaches "the banks of the great grey-green, greasy Limpopo River." A group may get nervous, however, if you periodically appear to be in danger of falling off your chair because you haven't "caught your breath."

Above all, aim for an understandable delivery. Some regional accents, for instance, can confuse listeners not used to hearing such patterns. A high- or very low-pitched voice sometimes accents regional differences and makes it hard to listen. A reader may be unaware of such voice qualities, but a session or two with a tape recorder will certainly identify problem areas. More careful enunciation will modify most problems. Clear enunciation, in fact, helps with all aspects of reading aloud. This does not mean such exaggerated pronunciation that words "hang like ice cubes in the air," as critic Aidan Chambers describes it. Careful attention to the endings of words and sentences, however, helps the listeners to pay attention to the story, not to your reading style.

Finally, there is that bit of polish that makes reading sessions something special. It is the confidence that comes with practice and experience. There is no substitute for enthusiasm and preparation—but it does get easier with practice. One gradually becomes more aware of a story's possibilities and of an audience's subtle reactions. The experienced reader knows that a pause just before Hobberdy Dick makes his choice between the green suit of antic mirth and the red suit of humanity heightens the drama and allows the audience just that second to anticipate the satisfaction of the "right choice." The skilled reader knows that a lowered voice can emphasize the foreshadowing of events as Old Da tells Robbie the legend of the Great Selkie in *A Stranger Came Ashore*.

You will be well rewarded for polishing your skills —by the clamor for "just one more" or the nearly silent sigh of satisfaction.

IV/What to Read?

**140 BOOKS RECOMMENDED FOR READING
ALOUD TO CHILDREN OF ELEMENTARY AND
MIDDLE SCHOOL AGE**

> *We offer this list of books with something
> of the pleasure that a matchmaker must
> feel when she or he brings together the
> perfect couple. . . .*

All right. You're sold on the value of reading aloud;
you *will* make time to read to the children in your life,
by hook or by crook. And you've picked up some tips
that will make you an effective reader-aloud. Just one
question remains: *what to read?* You've heard of a few
books that are rousing successes when read aloud—
E. B. White's *Charlotte's Web,* for instance. But beyond *Charlotte's Web,* a blank.

Perhaps you have tried books you remember from
your own childhood and have been dismayed to discover how dry many passages of *The Leatherstocking
Tales* seem now or how syrupy-sweet *The Five Little
Peppers.* Even the fondly remembered *Beautiful Joe*
turns out to be too sentimental for today's tastes. We
know one father whose attempt to read *Robinson
Crusoe* to his ten-year-old was abandoned by mutual
consent after about twenty minutes, for though children still love survival tales, they no longer have to
wade through hundred-word sentences and pious
moralizing to get them. In short, your good intentions
are frustrated by not knowing which of the old books

retain their appeal or what good books for children have been published since you were a child.

Or it may be that as a teacher you chose to read a book by an author you know to be popular with children. When you got into it, you discovered that the book is written from a child's point of view and expressed in a child's voice. You felt like a phony reading: "This kid who moved into my building is unreal, I tell you—I mean *weird*." Besides, the language gained nothing by being read aloud—in fact, oral reading probably revealed that the language and style were the book's weakest elements. Pell-mell plot and appealing characters can often sustain a silent reading but are unlikely to prevent a book that lacks other qualities from falling flat when read aloud.

For this part of the guide, then, we have culled from hundreds of titles those we believe will be successful when read aloud, and rewarding to both reader and listener.

The criteria on which our recommendations are based are strict. The books on this list differ from most lists of recommended titles in that they *read well aloud*. Many of them we ourselves have read to living, squirming children and found that they worked. The squirmers became still, the next installment was eagerly awaited, and children frequently went on to reread the book or to read others by the same author.

We tried to include a good number of *books that children might not pick up and read for themselves*. We agree with Aidan Chambers's principle that the limited time available for reading aloud should be weighed "in favor of those books that children need help with in order to find the pleasure they offer" (*The Horn Book Magazine* [February 1981], 107). This doesn't mean that there aren't many readily accessible books on the list, however, and these are good choices to start with. (They have been listed as "Surefire Books" in Chapter V.)

The books we have chosen *work well with groups* as small as a family of three and as large as an entire class. They are also books that lend themselves to being shared between adults and children. Many books which are popular with pre-adolescent children in particular explore experiences and feelings that are private and not intended to be shared with an adult or even with a group of children. The atmosphere of intimacy on which their appeal hinges is violated by having an adult reader stand between the story and the child, so to speak. Judy Blume, whose books are obvious examples of this type, confided to an interviewer: "I shudder sometimes when a teacher or librarian tells me that she's reading these books out loud because I really feel they're personal books. They're personal experiences, just between me and the child who's reading them" (James A. Smith and Dorothy M. Park, *Word Music and Word Magic* [Boston: Allyn and Bacon, 1977], 280).

The books on our list are titles that we judge to be *high in literary value*. Some would assume that this means we have simply produced yet another list of the standard classics, but we do not agree with those who see the classics of the past as superior to anything written in our own day. Our recommendations include both the literature of the past and recent books that

we judge outstanding. This emphasis on literary quality means that no book made the list on the strength
of its message alone, whether it be teaching children
native American customs, showing them the value of
honesty, or warning of the dangers of peer pressure.
The recommended titles may communicate many sorts
of information and values to children, of course, but
they earn a place on the list only if they are outstanding literature, shaping and communicating human experience in such a way as to illuminate, move, or
delight the listener.

One of the qualities of outstanding literature is that
it enhances one's sense of human possibility in some
way. We have recommended no book that we think
would injure the self-esteem of a child or reinforce a
biased view of those in some way different from the
listener. Some books with strong stories and definite
reader appeal were not included because the bias of
another time seems to pervade them. That does not
mean, however, that we rejected any book that depicts
a prejudiced character or idea. When racist or sexist
attitudes are expressed in dialogue or situation as a
way of characterizing a person or a whole society, but
do not represent the attitudes of the author (as de-
duced from the book as a total experience), we have
no objection to the book. One criterion of good historical fiction, after all, is that it be an accurate depiction of past ideas and attitudes; such stories can help
children understand the roots of prejudice in the past.

In reading aloud, when you come upon prejudiced
remarks used to characterize a person or time, you
may want to make clear that this is not your view. For

instance, several of our otherwise unobjectionable books portray young boys as thinking or saying, "Oh, she's only a girl!" Children are smart enough to know that the author's intention isn't to denigrate females but to create a specific and believable boy who is at the stage where he has to bolster his own confidence by putting down the other sex. A shake of the head and a roll of the eyes may be sufficient to let listeners know that you view such a remark as silly.

More discussion may be needed when reading aloud a book like *Sounder*. With the stark simplicity of traditional folklore, this poignant tale relates the sufferings of a poor black sharecropper's family decades ago. The cruelties of the bigots and the courage of the protagonist and his family are depicted in their actions, but the narrator does not explicitly condemn the one and praise the other. Talking about the story can assure that all the children clearly perceive where the author's sympathies and respect lie. Young listeners also need to be reminded that in the early part of the twentieth century, black Americans had fewer avenues by which to protest against and resist injustices. We need to supply historical perspective lest today's children unfairly dismiss these heroic characters as unduly passive.

Some outstanding books do not appear on the list because we felt they might be too painful or upsetting for a sensitive child (Paula Fox's *The Slave Dancer* is one such book). While we believe that most children, especially from about the age of ten on, are able to deal with harsh truths of life as well as (or better than) many adults, and while we applaud writers courageous enough to explore these subjects, we see a difference here between the experience of independent reading and that of listening to a book as a member of a group. Children are very good judges of what their psyches can handle. If a book that they have chosen and are reading to themselves makes them uncomfortable, they will stop reading it. But children being read to—particularly in the school situation—are a captive audience. They can't leave; most are reluctant to admit that they are scared or upset by the story. Thus, in selecting books to be read aloud to a group, we have been more cautious than we would be in recommending books for independent reading. In general, we suggest that the larger or less familiar the audience, the more conservative one should be when it comes to selecting potentially disturbing material.

Other fine books that we omitted don't lend themselves to oral presentation because they cannot be appreciated unless the reader has the page right in front of her or him. In some such cases, detailed illustrations must be examined simultaneously with the text. In others, charts, diagrams, or handwritten notes play a major part in the book's meaning (Ellen Raskin's engaging puzzle-mysteries fall into this category).

Although availability of books was an important consideration, we have included a few books that are currently out of print, noting that fact in the heading of that listing. These books, which were too good to leave out, should be available in many libraries.

We decided to include only one entry for each author so that we could provide a broader selection of writers. If you have had great success with a book, by all means seek out additional titles by the same author.

You will find on the list books to suit different ages, tastes, and situations. Although we encourage regular repeated sessions for sharing "chapter books" with children, we know that sometimes a reader can't be sure of getting an audience back again soon, or just may feel like reading a complete story in one sitting. For such occasions we have included "thin books," just right for one reading session, and collections of ancient folktales and contemporary short stories, any one of which can provide a complete literary experience in a few minutes. On the other hand, if you or your listeners hate to have a good thing come to an end, there are a few novels that will stretch over weeks.

The list is balanced between stories featuring female characters and those focusing on male characters. We strongly discourage teachers from choosing only "boys' books" for reading to a mixed group of girls and boys. In the past many teachers and librarians were advised to do this because of the antiquated notion that girls will read about boys but boys won't read (or listen to) a book about girls. This may have been true when so-called boys' books were much more exciting than the insipid volumes labeled "girls' books," but with the lively and interesting books published in recent years featuring female protagonists, it is no longer the case. Both boys and girls will enjoy and profit from imaginatively sharing the experiences of a member of the other sex.

Comedy, romance, adventure, biography, historical

fiction, and fantasy are all represented in our listings, as well as a few informational books of outstanding literary qualities. We encourage you to build a similar variety into your reading-aloud plans.

We offer this list of books with something of the pleasure that a matchmaker must feel when she or he brings together the perfect couple: we believe you'll find books here that will become a cherished part of your and your listeners' lives.

A Note on Suggested Listening Levels

The "Suggested Listening Level" that follows each book's annotation is a rough estimate of the grade span for a potential audience. Children who have been read to a great deal and are eager listeners may be ready for a particular book much earlier than we've indicated. Our estimates refer to the typical child and can be applied more directly when reading to children in the school than in the home. The better you know the child or children to whom you will be reading, the more you can substitute your own judgment for ours.

Our suggested grade levels tend to be lower than the reading levels publishers or reviewers use to indicate how much difficulty a book will pose to the child reader. Because these books are to be read *to* children, we have aimed at matching books to the interests and general understanding of children at particular ages, not to reading skills.

For family reading, we recommend choosing a book geared more to the older children's level and interests. Parts of the book may be over the head of a younger child in the family, but she or he will take from the story that which is meaningful and feel proud to be offered a more grown-up story, while an older child won't stay around long for a book that is aimed at younger children. (A list of books we think will hold the interest of children of different ages, headed "Wide Age-Range," appears in Chapter V.)

Abel's Island BY WILLIAM STEIG. *Illustrated by the author*. New York: Farrar, Straus & Giroux, 1976. Paperback: Bantam Books, 1977.

Abel's Island recounts the harrowing adventures of a mouse who, in the midst of a picnic, is swept away from his beloved bride by a sudden storm. He ends up on an uninhabited island in the midst of a river. The dangers Abel encounters in the months that follow— near-drowning, owls, starvation, despair—are sometimes scary, sometimes comical, but always interesting.

Steig eloquently chronicles the stages of Abel's transformation from a dandified and somewhat shallow city
fellow to a self-sufficient individual who has con-
fronted the fundamental philosophic questions as well
as the practical issues of life.

The author is a cartoonist for *The New Yorker* magazine and the book's illustrations are outstanding, but
clearly Steig has been influenced by *The New Yorker*'s
distinguished prose stylists as well, for all his children's
books are polished and original in expression with
cadences tailor-made for reading aloud.

As one might guess from the loving mouse-husband's
full name, Abelard, there are many allusions in the
book that will amuse well-read adults and older children. Yet the story is equally satisfying to those who
experience it simply as a Crusoe tale of intrepid victory
against great odds. Thus it is a good choice for a
family with a wide range of ages.

The book's twenty chapters average five minutes'
reading time, so the total book can be read aloud in
just under two hours. Steig's shorter animal fantasies
are good choices for younger children, five to eight
years old. *The Amazing Bone, Sylvester and the Magic
Pebble,* and *Caleb and Kate* are our favorites.

Suggested Listening Level: Grades 4–8

**About Wise Men and Simpletons: Twelve Tales from
Grimm.**   TRANSLATED BY ELIZABETH SHUB.   *Illustrated
by Nonny Hogrogian.*   New York: Macmillan, 1971.

This attractive volume contains some of the best
known of the folktales collected by the Grimm brothers:
"The Elves and the Shoemaker," "Briar Rose" (a

Sleeping Beauty tale), "Hansel and Gretel," and "The Bremen Town Musicians." Here, too, are a few less familiar but deeply appealing stories, especially in the section "About Simpletons." The language throughout is spare, the rhythm flowing, and, as the introduction points out, "the storyteller's voice is omnipresent."

These are translations without the embellishments that other adaptations offer, short and to the point of the story. They provide easy reading for bedtime or for the last ten minutes before the bus comes. Primary grades will enjoy every minute, and older listeners usually don't mind being reminded of their old favorites.

(Readers should know that the "Rapunzel" in this volume is not the familiar "toned down" version. Here the witch finds out about the prince's visits to the tower when Rapunzel wonders out loud why her clothes are getting tight and the witch sees that she is pregnant.)

Suggested Listening Level: Grades K–6

Across Five Aprils BY IRENE HUNT.   New York: Follet Publishing Company, 1964. Paperback: Grosset & Dunlap, Ace Books, 1981.

In April 1861, all the talk in rural southern Illinois is of imminent war—talk that makes Ellen Creighton fearful that her grown sons will be lost as were her three little boys in an epidemic years before. But to her youngest child, nine-year-old Jethro, war means loud brass music and men on shining horses—and he's impatient with President Lincoln's wavering. When war comes, it brings to the farm pain Jethro never imagined. By the next April, one brother is among the Union dead at Pittsburg Landing. Another brother, Jethro's favorite, follows his conscience and joins the Confederate Army. This provokes a gang of rowdies to contaminate the Creighton well and burn the barn. Jethro must take on a man's work, his childhood snatched away long before the armistice is signed. The book ends on a comforting note as Jethro's dream of an education promises to come true, but it is a sober rejoicing indeed.

Through the skillful use of authentic detail, Irene Hunt depicts the scene and characters so vividly that *Across Five Aprils,* set far from any battlefield, provides a clearer sense of the meaning and impact of the Civil War than any other book for children. Each of the twelve chapters supplies ample material for one reading session.

Suggested Listening Level: Grades 5–8

The Adventures of Tom Sawyer BY MARK TWAIN (pseud. Samuel Langhorne Clemens). 1876. Many editions.

The Adventures of Tom Sawyer still has great vitality and appeal to children, though weighted down a bit with nostalgia and satire of bygone institutions. Twain's account of boyhood in an earlier era has lavish amounts of two surefire ingredients: humor and suspense. Whether Tom is playing with a pinch-bug in church, dosing Aunt Polly's cat with pain-killer, or collecting valuables from his friends for the privilege of whitewashing the fence, his shenanigans amuse listeners of all ages. The suspense begins to build when

Tom and Huck witness a murder and culminates when Tom and Becky Thatcher discover that they are lost in the great cave with Injun Joe, the murderer.

Some sections are digressions from the exciting plot and you may want to do some slight editing—shortening the examples of "youthful eloquence" (i.e., school recitations) in chapter twenty-one, for instance. The stereotyping of Injun Joe should be pointed out to children as a common, but unfortunate, attitude in nineteenth-century America. The thirty-five chapters vary in length; we recommend taking a cue from your audience's interest when deciding how many chapters to include in a particular reading session.

Suggested Listening Level: Grades 4–8

The Alfred Summer BY JAN SLEPIAN. New York: Macmillan, 1980. Paperback: Scholastic Book Services, 1981.

Told by Lester, whose cerebral palsy makes him look "like a puppet whose manager has been goosed by lightning," this is a remarkable story of determination and the ability of the human spirit to rise above limiting circumstances. Tied to his mother by invisible strings, Lester is friendless and ignored, an object of pity or scorn, considered unable to do anything on his own. Then he meets Alfred, a skinny kid with black curls, dark eyes, and "nothing going on inside or outside." But Alfred accepts Lester as he is, makes no demands, and when Lester helps rescue Alfred at the beach, a friendship is begun.

These two are joined by lumpy, red-faced Myron, who is also beleaguered by mother, sisters, assorted relatives, and neighbors. Myron has a secret dream that he finally shares with Lester and Alfred: He is building a boat in the basement of his Brooklyn apartment house. Claire, a fast-talker who is also a sympathetic listener, completes the group, and the four begin building not only a boat but relationships that provide a sense of independence and a realization that each one has something special to contribute.

The hope and tough-mindedness of these characters will allow young listeners to understand the feelings locked in an uncooperative body. While the story can be read in about two and a half hours, the characters remain unforgettable.

Suggested Listening Level: Grades 5–8

Alice's Adventures in Wonderland   BY LEWIS CARROLL (pseud. Charles L. Dodgson). *Illustrations by John Tenniel.* 1865. Many editions.

Lewis Carroll's classic is a book that we recommend with reservations. Without question it was a historical milestone in the development of children's books. And many adults have reported that they were deeply and happily affected by it as children. Yet we know more than a few children who intensely dislike the book—*and* its celebrated Tenniel illustrations.

We can only guess at the reasons for such different responses, but it seems likely that some children are upset by Alice's confusion and anxiety through much of the story. Her adventures in Wonderland are not a pleasant experience for her, by and large, even though her awakening at the end shows that the threats were not real. Children who like the book seem to respond to its humor and to the wonder of a world in which one can shrink as well as grow, of babies that turn into pigs, and of just plain nonsense. They notice that Alice is really superior to all those zany adult figures and relish her eventual rebellion against their endless rules.

Even children who enjoy the book do not enjoy every episode equally, though. The size-changing bits fascinate children of five and six, while appreciation of the parody of Victorian educational practices requires a more mature listener. And then the humor of some episodes loses its point because it depends on a knowledge of English history or of songs and events of Carroll's own day.

We recommend, then, that you read aloud the early chapters, "Down the Rabbit Hole" and "The Pool of Tears," and then continue only if the reception has been enthusiastic. If you do read on, continue to gauge your listeners' interest and omit sections that seem tedious. Even if you read only the opening chapters, you will have introduced children to a work of literature that has permeated our culture, and stretched their imaginations. For those children who become Carroll devotees, *Through the Looking Glass* offers more adventures of Alice. Each book consists of twelve chapters.

Suggested Listening Level: Grades 1–5

All-of-a-Kind Family BY SYDNEY TAYLOR. *Illustrations by Helen John.* Chicago: Follett Publishing Company, 1951. Paperback: Dell, 1981.

In this book, Sidney Taylor chronicles the everyday

life of a Jewish family on Manhattan's Lower East Side in the early twentieth century. The episodes have the homey warmth and gentle humor that primary-grade children love in family stories. Each of the five sisters, ranging from four to twelve, has a different personality; most children find the dramatic, head-strong Henny especially interesting.

The episodes revolve around situations all children experience—losing a library book, trying to spend one's allowance wisely at the candy store, feeling left out when one's siblings are sick. At the same time, the author faithfully re-creates the distinctively Jewish ambience of her childhood. Holiday customs, foods, and the colorful world of pushcarts and little shops are described clearly and provide a good introduction to immigrant life for both Jewish and non-Jewish children.

The thirteen chapters vary in length but each is a self-contained episode and should be read in one session. This book has several sequels.

Suggested Listening Level: Grades K–3

American Tall Tales BY ADRIEN STOUTENBURG. *Illustrated by Richard M. Powers.* New York: The Viking Press, 1966. Paperback: Penguin, 1969.

Here are the stories of eight brave men, strong and true: Paul Bunyan, Pecos Bill, Stormalong (Alfred Bulltop Stormalong, that is), Davy Crockett, Johnny Appleseed, John Henry, and Mike Fink. They lived in the days when America was new and "trees were there, stretching in tall, wind-shining rows"; when Texas had "so much sky that it seemed as if there couldn't be

any sky left over for the rest of the United States."
And each one of these heroes was mighty big. Davy
Crockett was never *quite* as tall as the Great Smoky
Mountains, but nearly so. Stormalong, they say, was
nearly two fathoms high by the time he was ten. Since
a fathom is about six feet, "Stormy was pretty tall."
And Mike Fink spoke for all of them when he said,
"I'm second cousin to a hurricane, first cousin to a
seven-day blizzard and brother to an earthquake!"

The author has handled the folklore material with
the ease of a scholar and the ear of a storyteller. The
language reflects a time when gigantic tasks challenged
the ingenuity and taxed the stamina of men and
women. These exaggerations are most appreciated by
listeners of at least fourth grade level. Too many of
these tales read in succession could wear thin, however, so we recommend interspersing them with other
stories.

Suggested Listening Level: Grades 4–7

Anastasia Again!   BY LOIS LOWRY.   Boston: Houghton Mifflin Company, 1981.   Paperback: Dell, 1982.
Anastasia is afraid that when her family moves from
Cambridge, Massachusetts, to the suburbs (ugh!) her
mother will take to wearing big pink curlers and
worrying about wax buildup. But when the family
sees their new house, they fall in love with it because
it has everything: a study with bookshelves floor to
ceiling for her English-professor father; a solarium for
her painter mother; plenty of closets for two-year-old
Sam (he likes standing in them); and for Anastasia—
a tower! Even with the move finished, however,

Anastasia must begin the difficult task of finding new friends.

Another ordinary move-into-the-new-neighborhood-find-a-friend story? Wrong. There is absolutely nothing ordinary about Anastasia Krupnik—from father to friends. And rarely will you find a funnier party than the one Anastasia arranges with the local senior citizens' "Drop-in Center" for her next-door neighbor, Mrs. Stein. For families who also read *The New York Review of Books,* for classrooms who don't mind a bit of irreverent hilarity, *Anastasia Again* will provide approximately three and a half hours of side-splitting delight. To get through the party scene, though, the reader *must* prepare—otherwise your audience will never be able to hear the story through your own laughter. *Anastasia Krupnik* is an earlier book about the Krupnik family. It is appealing but not quite as funny as *Anastasia Again.*

Suggested Listening Level: Grades 5–8

. . . and Now Miguel   BY JOSEPH KRUMGOLD.   *Illustrated by Jean Charlot.*   New York: Thomas Y. Crowell Company, 1953.   Paperback: Crowell, Apollo Editions, 1970.

This coming-of-age story focuses on Miguel Chavez, an often overlooked child in the middle of a large family of sheep ranchers. Twelve-year-old Miguel wants passionately to go to the Sangre de Cristo mountains in the summer with the men and the flocks but is told he's too young. He decides to work so hard and well that his father will change his mind. The book is narrated from Miguel's point of view, and his desperate longing is convincingly rendered, as is the close relationship between Miguel and his adored older brother. Krumgold succeeds in creating a touching portrait that all children will understand.

The story depicts in detail the culture of New Mexican sheep ranchers, a fascinating way of life that goes back centuries to Spain. Each of the fourteen chapters is an interesting episode in Miguel's ultimately successful campaign, but the narration is leisurely and contemplative. This is not a book for wigglers or easily distractible children. The distinguished illustrations by a noted muralist and painter add authenticity to the story.

Suggested Listening Level: Grades 4–6

And Then What Happened, Paul Revere? BY JEAN FRITZ. *Illustrated by Margot Tomes.* New York: Coward, McCann & Geoghegan, 1973. Paperback: Coward, McCann & Geoghegan, 1982.

Paul Revere was a man of many talents. When he took over his father's silversmithing business, he made everything from beads to candlesticks. He even made a silver collar for a pet squirrel. But more than that, he rang church bells, went off to fight in the French and Indian War, and became a leader in the secret Sons of Liberty.

This is a spirited biography, full of the life and times of an active man and his exciting Boston-town. The style is lively and the questions posed by the author— "What could be done?" "So what happened?" "And *then* what happened?"—serve to point up the action. This could be read in one long session (probably about forty minutes) for primary grades but would break easily about midway through as Paul Revere is declared the Number One express rider between Boston and Philadelphia (page 23). The book should be made available to children after it is read aloud so that they can enjoy the details of Margot Tomes's vigorous illustrations. Many of the author's other witty biographies are also good for reading aloud.

Suggested Listening Level: Grades 2–4

The Animal Family BY RANDALL JARRELL. *Illustrated by Maurice Sendak.* New York: Pantheon Books, 1965.

The hunter lived in a cabin that he had made, surrounded by the skins of animals that he had caught for cap and coat and rug. But in the spring when "the beach was all foam-white and sea-blue with flowers" and in the winter "when a great green meteor went slowly across the sky," there was no one to tell what he had seen. Then one summer evening the hunter heard the song of the mermaid and he waited and watched and courted her, patient as the animals he knew so well. They taught each other words and spent time in the meadow, and in the fall she went into the house.

A bear cub, a lynx, and finally a baby boy join the hunter and the mermaid in their lyrical life. The images are so vivid that both reader and listener will want to savor every word. Maurice Sendak's delicate line drawings depict only the physical setting of this special place, leaving one with the impression that the characters are just off the edge of the page. Don't make this a first choice and don't rush the experience. "Plot" and "action" are terms that don't apply, but "poetry," "music," "imagination" do. Find a place where the forest runs down to the ocean, for "say what you like, but such things do happen—not often, but they do happen."

Suggested Listening Level: Grades 3–8

April Morning BY HOWARD FAST. New York: Crown Publishers, 1961. Paperback: Bantam Books, 1981.

The frontispiece in one edition of this book, seeking to catch the reader's attention, trumpets "*April Morning*: a novel about one of the most glorious days in American history," but the true achievement of Howard Fast's book is to reveal the total absence of glory at Lexington and Concord on April 19, 1776. This first-person account of that day and the preceding one does much more than depict a historical event. It explores the nature of courage, of grief, and of the fear of death, as experienced by a fifteen-year-old boy who faced the British on Lexington green, saw his father shot, fled in panic, and then sniped at the Redcoats as they marched back to Boston. Adam's physical and emotional states are tellingly captured, making this an honest and eloquent addition to American coming-of-age fiction.

Readers must be prepared to encounter unpleasant descriptions of what wounds actually look like, but none are gratuitous and to omit them from realistic battle accounts would be dishonest. Unlike some historical novelists writing for the young, Fast does not suggest an easy distribution of right and wrong. His faithfulness to life's complexities anticipates the carefully documented fiction of the Collier brothers (especially *My Brother Sam Is Dead*), but *April Morning* is better suited to reading aloud.

The novel is divided into eight sections; if you can devote a half hour or so at a stretch to reading, we recommend completing one section at a sitting.

Suggested Listening Level: Grades 6–8

Aunt America BY MARIE H. BLOCH. *Illustrated by* JOAN BERG. New York: Atheneum, 1963. Paperback: Atheneum, 1972.

The arrival of an aunt from America to visit her nephews and their families throws their small Ukrainian village into an excited turmoil. Eleven-year-old Lesya can hardly wait to meet her "Aunt America," but the visit turns out to be a painful time for her. To begin with, she is terribly disappointed in her gift from America. Then, too, Aunt Lydia seems to prefer Lesya's father to her Uncle Vlodko. Lesya has always been ashamed of her parents because they were arrested and imprisoned by the Russian secret police for supporting the Ukrainian independence movement. After their return, she often found herself wishing that her father would behave properly, like Uncle Vlodko. Through Aunt Lydia, Lesya comes to appreciate her father's courage and integrity and to see that her uncle's worldly success and ability to get along with officials are signs of weakness. The suspense builds as Lesya performs a courageous act of her own, traveling all the way to Kiev to warn her aunt of impending danger.

This glimpse of life in the Soviet Union grew out of a visit the author made in 1960 to her native village in the West Ukraine. Though the story conveys a thought-provoking glimpse of life in an authoritarian state, it is above all a good story, suspenseful and tuned in to universal childhood experiences.

To understand the story, children need to know that the Soviet Union is formed of many distinct national groups that were incorporated into one authoritarian state, dominated by the Russians. *Aunt America* consists of fourteen short chapters. Total reading time is approximately two and a half hours.

Suggested Listening Level: Grades 4–6

A Bear Called Paddington BY MICHAEL BOND. *Illustrated by Peggy Fortnum.* Boston: Houghton Mifflin Company, 1960. Paperback: Dell, 1968.

Mr. and Mrs. Brown found the bear in Paddington Station "a very unusual kind of bear. It was brown in colour, a rather dirty brown, and it was wearing a most odd-looking hat, with a wide brim." The bear claimed that he was a stowaway from Darkest Peru, where he had been taught to speak English by Aunt Lucy before she went to the home for retired bears. Because he'd been discovered in the Station, the Browns called their bear Paddington. Things are never quite the same again in their London household, for Paddington in his shy, diffident way causes one disaster after another. Although *his* feelings are always soothed by some extra marmalade—Peruvian bears love marmalade—it is not as easy to calm the ruffled feelings of cooks or clerks or cabbies.

Paddington has become something of a celebrity, as his stuffed likeness appears in department stores and toy shops around the country. Anyone who has a replica of this jam-loving bear, however, should have the opportunity to meet the *real* Paddington in this first of the series. Two and a half hours' reading time should suffice, but those who have strong feelings about bears may demand repeats.

Suggested Listening Level: Grades K–4

Ben and Me   BY ROBERT LAWSON.   *Illustrated by the author.*   Boston: Little, Brown and Company, 1939. Paperback: Dell, 1973.

Amos, the oldest in a large family of poor church-mice, grows tired of nibbling at tough sermons and ventures out into the world, where he finds a warm refuge in the lining of Ben Franklin's fur cap. From this vantage point he finds he can advise the famous but rather inept Doctor Franklin on everything from inventions to statecraft to mud puddles that lie in the path. According to Amos, his ideas lead to the invention of the Franklin stove, although he lets Ben take the credit in return for supplying the comforts of life to Amos and his needy family. Amos's life from then on is never dull. He is nearly electrocuted as an unwilling subject in Ben's electricity experiments. Accompanying Ben to France, Amos organizes the daring rescue of a lovely French Mouse aristocrat.

Funny and irreverent, *Ben and Me* has long been a popular choice for reading aloud. Though it presupposes some knowledge of Benjamin Franklin's life, it is geared to the primary grades. We recommend in this case sharing Lawson's illustrations with the children as you go along; they add a great deal and are bold enough to be seen by a group. The adventures of Amos and Ben are recounted in fifteen chapters, each requiring about six to eight minutes of reading time.

Suggested Listening Level: Grades 2–4

Bert Breen's Barn   BY WALTER D. EDMONDS.   Boston: Little, Brown and Company, 1975.

Tom Dolan, going on nine years old, resolves to make life easier for his mother. As the daughter of one ne'er-do-well and deserted wife of another, she has lived in poverty all her life. By the time he is thirteen, Tom's determination "to turn around their lives" takes the form of vowing to earn enough to buy the Widow Breen's old barn and move it to their own place. Leaving school, Tom works at the local mill for twenty-five cents a day. With the help and advice of several adults who admire his industry, Tom's dream is finally realized.

Most of the account unfolds slowly and quietly, requiring of the listener a patience to match young Tom's. The suspense and action build toward the book's end, however, as Tom and his mother work in the dead of night to uncover Bert Breen's long-hidden life's savings before a gang of hoodlums arrives.

Though told in a laconic style, this tale of upstate New York in the early twentieth century is in the end deeply moving; we have come to know the characters so well that Tom's success becomes our own.

The book is a long one. Each chapter is only four or five pages long, but there are sixty-three of them, organized into seven parts.

Suggested Listening Level: Grades 4–8

The Borrowers BY MARY NORTON. *Illustrated by Beth and Joe Krush.* New York: Harcourt Brace and World, 1953. Paperback: Harcourt Brace and World, 1965.

Have you ever misplaced a needle, some stamps, a pencil or two, or a thimble? If these items or others unaccountably disappear, it is possible that the Borrowers are nearby. Borrowers are tiny people who live out of sight in old houses, subsisting on what they can "borrow" from "human beans." Cats or noisy children make life distinctly uncomfortable for them, and Routine and houses deep in the country are safest, but even in such circumstances there may be trouble. It certainly surprised Homily, Pod, and their daughter Arriety to find a Boy in the old house when none had been around for years. The Boy, however, provides the family with treasures beyond their dreams until the terrible day when the Borrowers are seen by Mrs. Driver, the housekeeper.

Listeners are fascinated by the miniature world of the Borrowers, perhaps because they too have noticed missing things and heard a rustle that can't be explained by a gust of wind. Once involved in the adventure of this intrepid family, you may wish to follow the Borrowers to their new homes in three other books. We find *The Borrowers Afield* the best of the sequels. The reading time for *The Borrowers* is approximately three hours, but be sure that the first session includes both chapters one and two so that the listeners have a chance to meet Pod, Homily, and Arriety and glimpse their world under the floorboards.

Suggested Listening Level: Grades 3–6

Bridge to Terabithia BY KATHERINE PATERSON. *Illustrated by Donna Diamond.* New York: Thomas Y. Crowell Company, 1977. Paperback: Avon Books, 1979.

Jess's life was hard enough, stuck in the middle of four sisters and loaded down with farm chores, without the new girl next door spoiling his dream of being the fastest runner in the fifth grade. In spite of himself, though, Jess begins to like Leslie, and before long they find a secret place that becomes their own private kingdom. Jess discovers he has much to learn about mythical kingdoms; he doesn't even know the proper language. The two youngsters teach each other, however, and Leslie shares with Jess her vivid imagination, her dreams, even her parents, who have left a busy city life for the isolated Virginia countryside. Jess attempts to protect Leslie from taunting classmates who can't imagine anyone living anywhere without television and begins to understand his own artistic talent for catching "the poetry of the trees."

There is much that is "usual" in children's books here: Two loners from different backgrounds find each other, become friends, grow up a bit. It is the author's deft characterization and understanding of the luminous quality of friendship, however, that brings this story out of the ordinary. Both Leslie and Jess are remarkably vivid people, and listeners will suffer with Jess at Leslie's tragic accident. The thirteen chapters are approximately ten to twelve minutes each. Longer sessions toward the end of the book may cushion the impact of Leslie's death with Jess's hopes for the future and the continuation of the kingdom of Terabithia. *The Great Gilly Hopkins,* also by Katherine Paterson, is the story of a feisty unwanted child, and is successful with children who have had a limited exposure to books.

Suggested Listening Level: Grades 4–7

The Bully of Barkham Street   BY MARY STOLZ.   *Illustrated by Leonard Shortall.*   New York: Harper & Row, 1963.   Paperback: Dell, 1968.

Martin Hastings, big for his grade, overweight, belligerent and a liar, is always in trouble. He picks on smaller kids, sasses adults, and drives away with his mean remarks anyone who tries to be friendly. We've all known a Martin Hastings, but Mary Stolz helps us see the world through his eyes. To Martin it seems that everyone is against him: his parents, who give away the dog who is his only friend; the kids who taunt him with names like Plump Pudding and Fatso; the teacher who ignores his imaginative composition to jump on spelling mistakes and inkblots. Gradually and believably over the course of the book, however, things improve for Martin, and we are left with that gift of good fiction—increased sensitivity to another person's experience.

The book is a companion volume to *The Dog on Barkham Street,* in which Mary Stolz recounts exactly the same events from the viewpoint of the younger boy next door, who is often the target of Martin's bullying. Both books display a rare understanding of children's feelings. If you can read both, begin with *The Dog on Barkham Street*. If you have time for only one, *The Bully of Barkham Street* is the more original and successful of the two books. The eight chapters run between twenty and thirty minutes each when read aloud.

Suggested Listening Level: Grades 3–6

Burnish Me Bright BY JULIA CUNNINGHAM. *Illustrated by Don Freeman.* New York: Pantheon Books, 1970. Paperback: Dell Books, 1980.

In a small French village a mute boy endures a miserable existence of frequent beatings and scanty food. Then he meets Monsieur Hilaire, who, though he is now old and ill, was "a few yesterdays ago" the greatest mime in the world. When the old man discovers that Auguste has the gift of mime, he teaches him in secret all that he can, and the boy's misery blossoms into happiness. Monsieur Hilaire dies, however, after warning the boy that to the suspicious villagers "the enemy is anyone who is different."

As this delicate tale unwinds the villagers come to fear Auguste's gift as witchcraft and he becomes the victim of mob violence. He survives, however, to keep alive the gift he has received from the old mime. In this story the author offers a parable about art and prejudice in a hostile world at a level children can understand. She creates the narrow society of a pro-

vincial village in deft strokes, and listeners will be
swept up in the current of impending tragedy. Fortunately, the love between Auguste and his mentor
plus the friends he finds among the children soften
the story's harsh events. Even so, this is not recommended fare for primary grades.

The entire book can be read in approximately an
hour and thirty minutes. The last two chapters, seven
and eight, are very short and should be read in the
same session. Don Freeman's graceful ink-and-wash
sketches capture the story's essence.

Suggested Listening Level: Grades 4–8

By the Great Horn Spoon!   BY SID FLEISCHMAN.   *Illustrated by Eric von Schmidt.*   Boston: Little, Brown
and Company, 1963.

Twelve-year-old Jack, an orphan, and Praiseworthy,
the family butler, stow away in potato barrels on a
vessel sailing around Cape Horn from Boston to California. The time is the height of the gold rush; their
object—to restore the family fortunes, of course. The
ingenuity and pluck of this delightful pair enable them
to extricate themselves and others from all sorts of
difficulties—they are becalmed, robbed, and bam-
boozled, among other things. Our heroes do strike it
rich, but then lose their gold. In the end, they manage
to solve the family's problems in an unexpected way.
You'll read many a book before you find one with as
satisfying an ending as this one. Though the story
smacks of the tall tale in its narrative style, it conveys
interesting and authentic information about gold rush
days, showing the rampant inflation in the gold fields,

for instance, and vividly describing the rotting ships that fill San Francisco harbor (they've been deserted by their gold-hungry crews).

This rollicking adventure yarn is a good choice for reading aloud. It is bound to please children and keep them clamoring for the next installment, but they might not choose it themselves because of its odd title. The book contains eighteen short chapters.

Suggested Listening Level: Grades 3–5

Calico Bush BY RACHEL FIELD. *Illustrated by Allen Lewis.* New York: Macmillan, 1931, 1966.

Calico Bush, a book written more than half a century ago (it was runner-up for the Newbery Medal in 1932), holds up remarkably well. It was reissued in 1966 and is still attracting a good many enthusiastic readers.

Marguerite Ledoux, who immigrated to America from France with her grandmother and uncle, found herself in the poorhouse after their sudden deaths. She had no choice but to become a "bound girl." The book opens in 1743 as she is traveling by boat to Maine from Marblehead, Massachusetts, with a poor family that has purchased her services for six years in return for giving her board and keep. Marguerite deals bravely with loneliness, endless chores, and the general prejudice against anything French, in addition to the hardships inherent in pioneering life. Her competence and courage through all sorts of crises make her a worthy and memorable heroine.

One needs to have a bit of French to do justice to this one in oral reading, for Marguerite frequently finds a French phrase slipping out at moments of emotion. Also, the words of a French lullaby play a part in a poignant episode.

Suggested Listening Level: Grades 4–7

Charlotte's Web BY E. B. WHITE. *Illustrated by Garth Williams.* New York: Harper & Brothers, 1952. Paperback: Harper & Row, 1974.

"Where's Papa going with that ax?" Fern's horror at her father's plans to kill the newborn runt pig rings out on the first page of *Charlotte's Web*. Fern prevails on her father to spare the pig, names him Wilbur, and raises him on a bottle until he's too big and must go to live in her uncle's barn down the road. The barn is a wonderful place, full of pleasant sounds and smells, but Wilbur is lonely until he makes a friend, a spider named Charlotte. In spite of her bloodthirsty way of life, Charlotte proves a loving and wise companion. It is she who conceives and executes the plan that saves Wilbur from being butchered in the fall.

If a vote were taken for the best-loved read-aloud book in America today, *Charlotte's Web* would win hands down. It has everything: humor, vivid characters, pathos (Charlotte, like all her kind, dies after laying her eggs), and wisdom. Though Charlotte's death will draw tears, White's sensitive handling of the subject provides reassurance on a level that children can grasp. Written by one of the finest prose stylists of our time, the book is a model of eloquent, yet simple, English language. Each of the twenty-two chapters makes a good read-aloud session for younger children; we strongly recommend, though, that you do not stop after chapter twenty-one (which ends with Charlotte's death), but read on as White describes the ways that Charlotte's spirit lives on.

Suggested Listening Level: Grades K–4

Cheaper by the Dozen BY FRANK B. GILBRETH AND ERNESTINE G. CAREY. New York: Thomas Y. Crowell Company, 1948. Paperback: Bantam Books, 1981.

The antics of the Gilbreth family keep children in stitches today just as they have for over thirty years. Life is never dull in a family of twelve children and two efficiency-expert parents. Much of the humor centers on Mr. Gilbreth, portly and a bit pompous but with a marvelous sense of humor. His trials include not only governing a crew of red-haired Irish kids who have inherited his gift for practical jokes, but coping with a temperamental Pierce Arrow (when cars were still a novelty). Mrs. Gilbreth is his foil—capable and serene through all the chaos. The Gilbreths' unconventional strategies for educating their brood, decades ahead of their time, give the book added substance.

Cheaper by the Dozen is ideal for family reading, as even young children can enjoy the slapstick elements, while mature listeners (and the reader) will appreciate the more subtle, irreverent touches.

The insensitivities of an earlier era crop up in two brief passages that you may want to edit or omit: a short minstrel-show routine near the end of chapter sixteen and the depiction of a stereotyped Chinese cook in chapter nine.

Suggested Listening Level: Grades 4–8

Child of the Silent Night: The Story of Laura Bridgman
BY EDITH FISHER HUNTER.   *Illustrated by Bea Holmes.*
Boston: Houghton Mifflin Company, 1963. Paper-
back: Dell, 1963.

Laura Bridgman had been blind and deaf since she
had scarlet fever at the age of two. Her friend Mr.
Asa Tenney, called Uncle Asa by the Bridgmans,
helped Laura and gave her the special love and attention she needed by taking her for long walks in the
woods so that she could touch and smell the life
around her. He explained it this way: "It is as though
Laura is living in a room without windows or doors.
I must make windows and doors into that room." Uncle
Asa's windows and doors were opened even wider for
Laura at the Perkins School for the Blind in Boston,
and she thrived in the environment provided her. This
biographical account does not minimize the hard work
and long hours spent by both Laura and her teachers
in mastering skills taken for granted by so many of us.

Primary grades listen and understand with sympathy
much of Laura's struggle. Total reading time is about
two hours, with chapters providing easy ten-minute
sessions. Although the action is minimal, even very
young listeners are captivated by the thoughtful Laura,
who asked what the wind was made of, and why a
waterfall doesn't stop.

Suggested Listening Level: Grades 2–3

Children of the Fox BY JILL PATON WALSH.   *Illustrated by Robin Eaton.*   New York: Farrar, Straus &
Giroux, 1978.

The three separate stories in this volume are linked

by the intriguing historical figure of Themistokles, an Athenian general who brought the Greek states safely through the Persian Wars, only to end in exile and disgrace. Children play the central role in each story, however, and events are narrated from their viewpoints. In this way, the author succeeds in drawing the young reader or listener into a world distant in time and space.

In the first story a sheltered young Athenian girl risks her life and good name to warn Themistokles of possible danger on the eve of the great sea-battle at Salamis. The second story depicts the devastation that faced the Greeks when they returned to Attica after the Persian occupation. Demeas finds a messenger who has broken his leg on the road and must take his place, running all the way to Sparta with a message of life-and-death importance to Themistokles. His reward is a bundle of olive saplings to replace the trees destroyed by the Persians. In the last story a young princess saves the life of the now discredited Themistokles.

Jill Paton Walsh has written many fine novels for young people, and it was difficult to decide which to include here. Short stories for children under twelve are hard to come by, however (except folktales), as is historical fiction that is accessible to children of varying abilities. On these counts, *Children of the Fox* recommends itself.

Each of the stories is roughly thirty pages long.

Suggested Listening Level: Grades 5–7

Childtimes: A Three-Generation Memoir BY ELOISE GREENFIELD AND LESSIE LITTLE. New York: Thomas Y. Crowell Company, 1979.

Children who like to hear about "olden days," who beg a parent or grandparent to "tell me about when you were little," will enjoy this memoir. The book consists of reminiscences by Eloise Greenfield—a black writer with many outstanding children's and adult books to her credit—by her mother, and by her grandmother. It is a moving chronicle of change in American childhood over a century and of the continuity provided by love and struggle that spans the generations. As the introductory section puts it: "There's a lot of crying in this book, and there's dying, too, but there's also new life and laughter. It's all part of living." The book's first two sections are set in and around the small hamlet of Parmelee, North Carolina; the third in Washington, D.C., for like many other black families, this one headed on north in 1929 to look for a safer and better life.

Childtimes lacks the suspense of fiction; the first part of the book, especially, consists of fragmented memories, and the events described are mostly undramatic, but they succeed in bringing to life people, involving us in their joys and sorrows. It is not a book to be read to a large group but is wonderful for family reading when children have grown old enough to be interested in learning more about life in the past. The book's design is unusually attractive with charcoal sketches and photographs of the authors' family.

Suggested Listening Level: Grades 5–8

The Chronicles of Robin Hood BY ROSEMARY SUT-
CLIFF. *Illustrated by C. Walter Hodges.* New York:
Oxford University Press, 1950, 1960 (out of print).

Robin Hood and his adventures have enthralled listeners in song and story since the late fifteenth century. Action and suspense abound as Robin, his Merry
Men, and his Lady fair are caught in the eternal
struggle of justice against tyranny, honor and love
against treachery and hate. Sutcliff is a historian who
understands the use of diverse sources, and she here
presents an account of Robin from the time he is
branded as an outlaw through his death.

Storytellers from balladeers to film-makers have provided children with interpretations of this legendary
figure. This one captures the timeless essence of the
story, without the pseudo-archaic language of many
versions. Each chapter can be read in twenty-five to
thirty minutes. Even younger listeners will understand
the poignancy of Robin's last wish for peace: "where
the arrow falls, that is where you shall bury me."

Suggested Listening Level: Grades 4–8

The Complete Peterkin Papers BY LUCRETIA P. HALE.
1880. *With original illustrations by the author.* Introduction by Nancy Hale. Boston: Houghton Mifflin
Company, 1960. Paperback: Dover Publications, 1960.

More than one hundred years have passed since
the Lady from Philadelphia first suggested to the
Peterkins—Mr. and Mrs. Peterkin, Agamemnon, Solo-
mon John, Elizabeth Eliza, and the three little boys in
their rubber boots—that they had only to turn the
piano around to avoid the inconvenience of playing it

through the porch window. Her touch of common sense serves again and again in these sketches to heighten the amusing absurdities of life in the Peterkin household, where the slightest difficulty always proves too much for the collective wits of the family.

These humorous stories have delighted listeners from Boston to San Francisco. Each episode is perfect for one sitting, although a group may have to be reminded about the role of the Lady from Philadelphia if much time has elapsed between readings. Audiences of a wide age-range enjoy the stories, but we recommend them especially for fourth and fifth grades, when the "bump" of humor seems to expand beyond the slapstick to appreciate the subtlety of exaggeration.

Suggested Listening Level: Grades 4–7

The Courage of Sarah Noble   BY ALICE DALGLIESH. *Illustrated by Leonard Weisgard.*   New York: Charles Scribner's Sons, 1954.   Paperback: Charles Scribner's Sons, 1954.

The only comfort for eight-year-old Sarah is her father's presence and the warm cloak her mother had fastened under her chin. In the dense forest, strange rustlings, real and imagined, seem almost overwhelming as she accompanies her father to a new home-site in eighteenth-century Connecticut. Most fearsome of all are the thoughts of Indians, until she meets the children of a village not far from the site of the Nobles' cabin. Sarah has need of all her courage, however, when her father leaves to bring the rest of the family back, asking her to remain with the Indian family of the man they call Tall John.

"Keep up your courage, Sarah Noble," was her mother's admonition as the journey began. It was a phrase that Sarah repeated over and over to herself and that listeners will pick up and share as the occasion demands. One youngster muttered it over and over to himself, substituting his own name, as he went to the hospital for a tonsillectomy. It can be read in two or three rather short sessions and is a good beginning for either kindergarten or first-grade listeners. The author's *Bears on Hemlock Mountain,* with its ringing refrain and exciting buildup of suspense, also makes good reading aloud.

Suggested Listening Level: Grades K–3

The Cow-tail Switch and Other West African Stories
BY HAROLD COURLANDER AND GEORGE HERZOG. *Illustrated by Madye Lee Chastain.* New York: Holt, Rinehart and Winston, 1962.

This volume contains eighteen varied stories of West African origin, among them forerunners of the Brer Rabbit stories of the American South and the Anansi stories of the West Indies. "Some of the stories make you think. Some make you laugh," the editor promises. "Kaddo's Wall," with its theme of the obligations of wealth, is one of the tales that provoke thought. Among those that evoke laughter are "Hungry Spider and the Turtle," a funnier version of Aesop's fox and crow fable, and the short and silly "Talk."

A note on the first story describes how the traditional African storyteller will often stop a story before the conclusion and ask the listeners what they think the outcome should be. You may want to try this with

"The Cow-tail Switch." Because some of the stories use different literary conventions than we are accustomed to, and because at least one is rather grim ("Anansi and Nothing Go Hunting for Wives"), we recommend the collection for the upper-elementary and middle school grades. The stories are accompanied by notes, a glossary, and a pronunciation guide that should prove helpful in preparing the stories.

Suggested Listening Level: Grades 4–8

The Cricket in Times Square   BY GEORGE SELDEN (pseud. George Selden Thompson). *Illustrated by Garth Williams.*   New York: Farrar, Straus & Giroux, 1960.   Paperback: Dell, 1970.

Transported unawares after feasting in a picnic basket, a Connecticut cricket named Chester finds himself stranded in the dirt and bustle of Times Square subway station. His chirping attracts friendly help, however, and soon he is snugly settled in the Bellinis' newsstand as the treasured pet of Mario Bellini. Tucker Mouse and Harry Cat, good-natured scavengers who live in a nearby drainpipe, also befriend Chester. When Chester discovers that he can learn and perform any piece of music he hears, Tucker is the one who sees a way to repay the kindness of the struggling Bellini family. In time, Chester's musical talent brings fame and modest fortune to the hardworking Bellinis.

All those who appreciate good music and good food, both younger and older audiences, will delight in the humor and solid sense of Tucker, Harry Cat, and, of course, Chester. This is an excellent choice for primary grades who have developed the ability to listen to longer narratives. We prefer to read the conversations between Mario and the Chinese gentleman Sai Fong without the somewhat exaggerated dialect indicated by the spelling ("Velly, velly good. You got clicket . . . You know stoly of first clicket?"). The author's skillful use of word order and diction are sufficient to characterize Mr. Fong. The fifteen chapters can be combined into about seven sessions, five if audiences can tolerate longer sessions.

Suggested Listening Level: Grades K–4

The Dollhouse Caper   BY JEAN S. O'CONNELL.   *Illustrated by Erik Blegvad.* New York: Thomas Y. Crowell Company, 1976.   Paperback: Scholastic Book Services, 1977.

Now that their home was off the high shelf and set up for the Christmas holidays, Mrs. Dollhouse should have been happy, but she couldn't help worrying. Would the young Humans, Kevin, Peter, and Harry, think themselves too grown up for Mr. and Mrs. Dollhouse and their family? And what about the robbery that the Dollhouse family overheard being plotted? How could the Humans be warned?

Like Father Dollhouse, who spends a lot of time stuffed headfirst in the dollhouse toilet by the middle brother, the assumption that doll stories are for girls is turned upside down by this book. The fast-paced account of how the Dollhouse family foil the robbers can't help but amuse both boys and girls, and boys will especially appreciate the author's understanding of the pressures on boys to grow up. The twelve chapters divide into six sessions of about twenty minutes each and provide surefire material for third through sixth grade.

Suggested Listening Level: Grades 3–6

Dragonwings   BY LAURENCE YEP.   New York: Harper & Row, 1975.

Dragonwings is the story of a Chinese immigrant to San Francisco who in 1909 successfully built and flew a biplane. It is based on fact, but nothing beyond this is known of the man. The book is Laurence Yep's attempt to flesh out the life of just one of the anonymous hundreds of thousands of Chinese who came to America in the nineteenth and early twentieth centuries. (Yep reports this in the afterword, but we've found that children prefer to know the story's relation to "real life" at the start.)

Events are described through the eyes of the inventor-flyer's young son, Moon Shadow. Throughout the book the non-Chinese reader is challenged to see Western culture from Moon Shadow's Chinese viewpoint, whether he is revolted by the awful greasy drink, cow's milk, or confronting a drunken mob of "red-and-white faces, distorted into hideous masks of hatred and cruelty." Moon Shadow's father, Windrider, has a dream of flying, however, that takes them both out of Chinatown, and in a "white demoness" and her granddaughter they find a measure of understanding and friendship.

The book does not gloss over unpleasantness: Moon

Shadow and his father visit graphically described opium dens in a violent underworld as they search for an addict relative, and the San Francisco earthquake reveals the moral depths to which some people sink in calamity. Moon Shadow and Windrider prevail, however, and the book is a fitting tribute to the unrecognized achievement of a brave and hardworking immigrant group that has greatly contributed to American society.

Child of the Owl, set in San Francisco's Chinese community in the 1970s, is another fine book by Yep about cultural identity and assimilation.

Suggested Listening Level: Grades 5–8

The Ears of Louis BY CONSTANCE C. GREENE. *Illustrated by Nola Langner.* New York: The Viking Press, 1974.

Louis had big ears and small muscles—a bad combination. This warm and funny novel tells how Louis comes to terms with his ears and with the constant teasing they invite. The problem is real but never overwhelming, for Louis has an understanding family, an elderly neighbor who gives him good advice over their fiercely competitive poker games, and a friend named Matthew who is everything a friend should be. "I think your ears are nice," he says. Why? "Well . . . when the sun shines through them, they're all pink and everything."

Constance Greene's own ears must be keen, for she captures just the way kids talk to each other and adults talk to kids, making this short novel great fun to read aloud. The book, which is divided into short sections, can be read in just over one hour.

Suggested Listening Level: Grades 3–5

The Egypt Game   BY ZILPHA KEATLEY SNYDER.   *Illustrated by Alton Raible.*   New York: Atheneum, 1967. Paperback: Atheneum, 1972.

April and Melanie, two friends with vivid imaginations, discover a chipped replica of the famous Nefertiti statue in an overgrown vacant lot behind a junkshop. Thus begins the Egypt game. They read about ancient Egypt, make costumes, and develop shrines and rituals for their secret world. Melanie's little brother, Marshall, plays too, as the crown prince of the ancient pharaohs, and three other children eventually join the "Egyptians." The murder of a child in the neighborhood, however, brings the Egypt game and all other outdoor play to an abrupt halt. To make things worse, the stern old "Professor" who owns the junkshop is a suspect in the murder. When April and Marshall are attacked by the murderer, however, it is the Professor who saves them and leads to the murderer's capture.

Each of the children in the story comes to life as a distinct and appealing person; that they happen to be of different races and nationalities (quite plausible in the California university-town setting) is a special bonus. The book consists of twenty-three chapters, with a total reading-aloud time of approximately four hours. The first chapter, which sets the scene, is a bit slow, so we recommend that the first reading session include chapter two. Once listeners are introduced in that chapter to April, with her Hollywood airs and great ideas, they'll be hooked.

Suggested Listening Level: Grades 4–7

The Endless Steppe BY ESTHER HAUTZIG. New York: Thomas Y. Crowell Company, 1968. Paperback: Scholastic Book Services, 1968.

The secure and lovely world of ten-year-old Esther Rudomin was destroyed one morning in June 1941 when Russian soldiers burst into her grandparents' home in Vilna, Poland. Arrested as capitalist "enemies of the people," Esther, her parents, and her grandparents travel in a cattle car with dozens of other prisoners for six miserable weeks to a frontier village on the Siberian steppe. There, under conditions of extreme hardship and deprivation, they work in a gypsum mine and on a farm. In spite of the suffering, the resilient young girl finds small pleasures—a rare American movie, visits to the bazaar in town, and eventually the beauty of the harsh, rugged steppes. She feels a real sense of loss, as well as deliverance, when the family is returned to Poland at the end of the war. There they discover that their exile has, ironically, saved their lives. The rest of the family has perished in Nazi concentration camps.

In this autobiographical account, Hautzig displays an excellent sense of pace, using telling incidents to convey emotion in an understated way. She captures the humanity of the characters so vividly that *their* strength gives us the strength to read on, and the book is ultimately a heartening, not a devastating, experience.

The book has twenty-two chapters. The first is quite long, plenty for one read-aloud session. Subsequent chapters can be read in combinations of two or three. Don't be intimidated by the occasional Russian or Polish place-name; just sound them out as you go. Listeners will be so caught up in the story that they won't be critical.

Suggested Listening Level: Grades 5–8

Escape from Warsaw   BY IAN SERRAILLIER.   Original title: *The Silver Sword. Illustrated by C. Walter Hodges.*   New York: S. G. Phillips, 1959.   Paperback: Scholastic Book Services, 1972.

When Joseph Balicki, headmaster of a Warsaw school, is imprisoned by the Nazis and his Swiss wife taken away for forced labor, their three children must depend on their own resources to survive the chaos of wartime Europe. They hide in bombed-out cellars in the winter and woods in the summer. Edek provides food and clothes until he, too, is captured and sent to Germany to work on a farm. Ruth and Bronia are joined by a ragamuffin named Jan as they begin their search for Edek and then their parents. It is Jan's "silver sword," a small letter-opener given him by Mr. Balicki, that becomes the symbol of hope that the children take with them all the way from Warsaw to Appenzell, Switzerland.

The story is based on a factual account, and in spite of incredible odds the children manage to find each other, stay together, and finally reach their parents. They experience terror and despair along the way, but this is not a depressing story—there is a degree of security in Ruth's strength and in the resourcefulness of Jan and Edek. The twenty-nine chapters can be read two or three at a time. Total reading time is about five hours.

Suggested Listening Level: Grades 4-6

A Fair Wind for Troy BY DORIS GATES. *Illustrated by Charles Mikolaycak.* New York: The Viking Press, 1976.

Daughter of Zeus, daughter of Leda, Helen was the most beautiful woman in the ancient world. When she chose Menelaus, one of the most powerful men in Greece, as her husband, all her other suitors took an oath swearing to exact no vengeance on the winner and to aid Menelaus should anyone ever abduct Helen. When the Trojan prince Paris stole her away, all of the warriors of Greece gathered under the leadership of Agamemnon to carry out their oath. Because of an offense to the goddess Artemis, however, the Greek ships are becalmed, and a sacrifice must be made to appease the goddess. Iphigenia, daughter of Agamemnon, is the price of "a fair wind for Troy."

The author has carefully chronicled the events leading to the Trojan War in this powerful retelling. You may wish to set the scene for this reading by discussing mythology in literature and by forewarning the listeners of the harsh and bloody events that are a part of this tradition. Gates has handled the story with the dignity and grandeur that it deserves, however, as she does in her other volumes of Greek mythology.

Each chapter has within it natural stopping points; twenty-minute sessions are usually enough, even for older listeners.

Suggested Listening Level: Grades 5–8

Fanny's Sister BY PENELOPE LIVELY. *Illustrated by Anita Lobel.* New York: E. P. Dutton & Co., 1980.

Fanny was the eldest and then there were Albert and Emma and Harriet and Charles and Jane and Susan—and now, a new baby! In the Victorian household where she lives, every minute of Fanny's day is ordered and she wishes more than once that there were no more babies. No more wailing, no more younger children to take her place on Nurse's lap. And then at church, she wishes once too often. Fanny panics when it appears that her prayer to have God take back the new baby just might come true.

This quiet, sedate story of everyday life more than a century ago is full of recognizable occurrences at every turn. It is comfortable and perfect for younger listeners up through third grade. While it could be read in one long sitting, approximately thirty to forty minutes, there is an appropriate break after Fanny discovers that the new baby is safe and before she decides to leave home.

Suggested Listening Level: Grades K–3

Fantastic Mr. Fox BY ROALD DAHL. *Illustrated by Donald Chaffin.* New York: Alfred A. Knopf, 1970. Paperback: Bantam Books, 1978.

Take three rich, greedy, and disgusting villains, pit them against a charming, clever fellow whose only crime is trying to feed his engaging family, and you have a story certain to appeal to primary-grade children—and their big sisters and brothers. Dahl's pellmell plot in which the three farmers Boggis, Bunce, and Bean destroy the countryside in their attempt to exterminate the fox family will capture children's attention immediately. The complete triumph of the fantastic Mr. Fox will leave them cheering.

Adults should be forewarned of Dahl's crude vulgarity. The villains pick their noses with filthy fingers, call each other rude names, and generally serve to set off by contrast the loving and mannerly hero.

This is flamboyant entertainment in the "Perils of Pauline" tradition, and Dahl is a master of it. The eighteen chapters are very short. Plan to read several in each session. Total reading time is under two hours.

Suggested Listening Level: Grades K–4

Five Children and It BY E. NESBIT (pseud. Edith Bland). *Illustrated by H. R. Millar.* London: Unwin, 1902; New York: Dodd, Mead, 1905. Paperback: Penguin Books, 1959.

When five brothers and sisters discover a Psammead while digging in the gravel quarry near their summer cottage, the stage is set for wondrous adventures. A Psammead, you see, is a sand-fairy, and this rather grumpy, Muppet-like creature is obliged to grant wishes that last until sundown. With their parents away, the children envision a perfectly blissful summer. Alas, they find their wishes often entail unpleasant consequences. When they request a quarryful of gold, the suspicious shopkeepers won't take their guineas and instead turn them over to the police. The wish for wings turns out well, as they enjoy a glorious day of flying around the countryside, but they are stranded, wingless, on a church roof at nightfall. Most disconcerting of all is Cyril's offhand wish that the troublesome baby would "grow up now." Before their eyes the two-year-old is transformed into a dapper young gentleman who views them as bothersome tagalongs.

Numerous writers since Nesbit have written similar fantasies, but they cannot duplicate her success, which owes a great deal to her perfectly gauged casual asides to the reader. For instance: "I know this is the second fight—or contest in this chapter, but I can't help it. It was that sort of day. You know yourself there are days when rows seem to keep on happening, quite without your meaning them to."

The slang is a bit dated (i.e., "brekker" for breakfast and pet names for all the children), and the English idiom may prove difficult for those inexperienced at reading aloud; nevertheless, the book retains its special charm across the years and cultures.

There are eleven chapters for the children's eleven adventures. The chapter "Scalps" embodies every dime-novel stereotype of American Indians, yet it is at heart a satire of the popular romanticized image of the Indian. (Check it out in advance and omit it if you find it objectionable.) Sequels are *The Phoenix and the Carpet* and *The Story of the Amulet*.

Suggested Listening Level: Grades 3–6

The Fledgling   BY JANE LANGTON.   New York: Harper & Row, 1980.   Paperback: Harper & Row, 1981.

Georgie was nine years old, a spindly wisp of thistledown looking more like six—or even five. The family was worried because Georgie wanted to fly; not just an ordinary wanting, but a determined wanting that included three attempts down the front stairs. And the great Canada goose on the seasonal flight southward wanted to find someone worthy of the special "present" he had found in Walden Pond. These two loners finally discover each other. Tucked close and safe on the goose's back, Georgie is at last flying! Through the night sky they glide—over the fields and woods, circling down toward Walden Pond. But their secret flying has not been so secret. Interfering Mr. Preek and Miss Prawn have seen the two and set out to "rescue" Georgie. The tragic result of their intervention ends Georgie's flying, but she will treasure forever the Goose's special present.

Who can say it's impossible? Certainly not the adults in this story; certainly not Eleanor or Edward, Georgie's cousins; certainly not readers/listeners of all ages. Since the spirits of Emerson and Thoreau permeate the story, this would be especially good for families traveling to the Boston area, but it could enthrall any group of listeners—third through sixth grades. Airplane travelers are also a natural audience for this book. The reader needs to be prepared for Langton's sometimes sudden changes of narrator.

Suggested Listening Level: Grades 3–6

Flying to the Moon and Other Strange Places BY MICHAEL COLLINS. New York: Farrar, Straus & Giroux, 1976.

In this autobiographical account of space exploration, Astronaut Collins reveals a thoughtful perspective
to young listeners. The first several chapters involve
his early life—he built model planes at nine—as well
as a short and fascinating account of the history of
rocketry. By chapter four the listener is involved in
more technical aspects of training as Collins and his
fellow astronauts struggle to absorb the complicated
and bewildering array of skills necessary to a space
pioneer. It is the Apollo 11 flight of the *Columbia* and
the lunar landing, however, that capture so much of
the listener's attention. You may decide to skip some
of the more technical aspects of this book, particularly
details of navigation. The last chapter, for instance, is
speculation about the direction of space exploration,
which has changed considerably in the years since this
was published. But for technically minded listeners of
fifth through eighth grades, this is a glimpse of a sensitive, thoughtful man that should be shared.

Suggested Listening Level: Grades 5–8

Fog Magic BY JULIA SAUER. *Illustrated by Lynd
Ward.* New York: The Viking Press, 1943. Paperback: Pocket Books, Archway Paperbacks, 1977.

Greta had always loved the fog. Her mother worried
about this fascination, but her father understood her
need to explore inside the gray blanket that often covered their part of the Nova Scotia shoreline, especially
Blue Cove. In the sunshine, when the water of the
inlet sparkled, Blue Cove was deserted with only the
shells of cellar holes left. But in the fog, when the
Tollerton horn called its warning, a village appeared

as it had been in the past. Greta met the Morrill family and found a best friend in Retha. She came to know the stories behind people and places taken for granted in the world outside the fog: the drowned sailors, the egg cup and silver spoon—and Princess the cat. All the life of the Cove was shared with her until her twelfth birthday, when, as her father said, "all things change and are put away to fold around you in years ahead."

This is a quiet, introspective story that is short enough to be read in three or four sessions and will entrance fourth- through sixth-grade listeners. Some adults may find the ending a bit too pat, but we've had good luck with this for fourth-graders, especially. Try it with Mollie Hunter's *A Stranger Came Ashore.*

Suggested Listening Level: Grades 3–6

From Anna BY JEAN LITTLE. *Illustrated by Joan Sandin.*   New York: Harper & Row, 1972.   Paperback: Harper & Row, 1973.

It isn't easy being the youngest in a family, especially when you feel awkward and ugly and much less clever than everyone else. Only Papa seemed to appreciate Anna, but even Papa had other things on his mind as the family prepared to leave Hitler's Germany and Papa's teaching post for a grocery store in Canada. There are many exciting experiences for the Solden family in their new home, but for Anna (and the listener) it is the discovery of her own worth that brings the story to life. As part of a routine physical examination, the doctor finds that Anna needs glasses and a special school. With Miss Williams and the other children in the class, Anna begins to "blossom and grow, just like a Christmas flower."

Anna's story is a warm, loving one told with humor and yet a good deal of action. There is a considerable amount of dialogue, but the story is very straightforward. A sequel to this story of the Soldens, *Listen for the Singing,* and several other books by the author are rewarding for reading aloud, such as *Mine for Keeps* or *Far from Home.* The chapters in *From Anna* are short and episodic, so that five or six sessions should finish the story. A word of warning: Anna is a child not easily forgotten. The audience will *demand* to hear more. And her story will bring tears to the audience and reader alike—keep the Kleenex handy.

Suggested Listening Level: Grades 3–5

From the Mixed-Up Files of Mrs. Basil E. Frankweiler BY ELAINE KONIGSBURG. *Illustrated by the author.* New York: Atheneum, 1967. Paperback: Dell, 1974.

When Claudia Kincaid gets fed up with the monotony of her suburban straight-A life, she decides to run away. Because she's a fastidious and organized child, she plans carefully and selects as her destination the Metropolitan Museum in New York. As companion she chooses her younger brother Jamie (he's rich enough to bankroll the expedition). Claudia and Jamie's successful adventure has all the appeal of Robinson Crusoe, and the elegant surroundings of the museum are a great improvement over any desert island. The children sleep in a sixteenth-century canopy bed, bathe in (and replenish their funds from) the museum fountain. Furthermore, their brains are challenged as they attempt to prove that a small statue on display is the work of the great Michelangelo.

Konigsburg uses a somewhat confusing frame device to tell the story: the narrator is wealthy art patron Mrs. Frankweiler, who is relating the children's adventures to her lawyer. The identity of the narrator becomes clear only gradually, however. For that reason the book is best read to experienced listeners. This Newbery Medal–winning novel will please Manhattan-lovers and museum-lovers as well as those who value originality in fiction.

Suggested Listening Level: Grades 4-6

The Golden Treasury of Myths and Legends   ADAPTED BY ANNE TERRY WHITE. *Illustrated by Alice and Martin Provensen.*   New York: Western Publishing Co., Golden Press, 1970 (out of print).

Greek and Roman myths, legends and epics of Theseus, Beowulf, Roland, Tristram and Iseult, Rustem and Sohrab, and Sigurd are included in this collection of ancient tales. The adaptations have been skillfully edited to provide the essence of the story while retaining the rhetoric of myth and legend. Tragedy and triumph are repeated refrains from a time when physical prowess was a mark of achievement. Children of ten and up respond deeply to the themes of human struggle and passion that have kept these tales alive for centuries.

Each of these adaptations can be read in its entirety, especially the more episodic myths, or in two or three sessions for the longer legends. *Beowulf* with its classic confrontation between man and monster holds middle school audiences spellbound long before they are ready to tackle a more complete translation independently.

Suggested Listening Level: Grades 4–8

The Good Master BY KATE SEREDY. *Illustrated by the author.* New York: The Viking Press, 1935.

Jancsi is excited about the visit of city-cousin Kate, but no one is quite ready for the "bag of screaming monkeys" that is the *real* Kate. Riding horses, climbing walls and hiding in the rafters, even planting flowers become adventures for the whole family as seen through the city-bred eyes of Kate.

Life and customs of the Hungarian countryside abound. Holidays are special times for the rural community, and the details are lovingly and faithfully included. There are four stories woven into the narrative that could be read separately, especially "The Little Rooster and the Diamond Button," which is included in many storytelling anthologies, or these stories could be included as presented. Strong-willed, energetic Kate loved the tales—and the tellers. Third- to fifth-grade audiences will be delighted to meet her.

Suggested Listening Level: Grades 3–5

The Great Brain BY JOHN D. FITZGERALD. *Illustrated by Mercer Mayer.* New York: The Dial Press, 1967. Paperback: Dell, 1971.

Otherwise known as Thomas Dennis Fitzgerald (T.D.), the Great Brain cannot resist moneymaking propositions, daring exploits, any challenge, even a swindle or two. His brother, J.D., relates these adventures of the Great Brain, his family, and his friends in turn-of-the-century Mormon Utah.

As a first-person account based on the childhood experience of the author, these humorous episodes can be read as individual stories or as part of a longer narrative. While many of the Great Brain's schemes are outrageous, his more thoughtful, sensitive nature emerges often enough to provide a depth of character that raises this and other titles in the series a step above merely "funny stories." Primary through middle grades will be intrigued by the Great Brain's solutions to problems. Warning: There may be an unacknowledged G.B. in the audience.

Suggested Listening Level: Grades 2–5

The Gull's Way BY LOUIS DARLING. *Photographs and illustrations by the author.* New York: William Morrow & Company, 1965.

A scientist-artist is deposited on a thirty-acre island, nine miles off the coast of Maine. Picking out a nesting pair of herring gulls from the thousands of breeding birds, he watches them from a blind for six weeks, recording in words, photographs, and sketches the brooding of the eggs, their hatching, and the early life of three gull chicks. The book is neither a strictly scientific account nor a fictionalized version of a gull's experience, "but the story of a few weeks in the lives of the watcher and the watched." What makes it an effective book for reading aloud is the fact that the watcher also can write; he is a superb essayist.

This would make an excellent introduction for children to field study of wildlife—with its account of the spartan conditions and of the interplay between the observer's feelings about "his" gull family and his commitment to rigorous scientific procedures in his study. Darling's explanation of how the very presence of the observer changes the behavior being studied is especially clear and effective. Although the text can stand on its own, all listeners will want to sit down at some point with the book to absorb the lovely sketches and photographs.

A quiet and contemplative book, this is not for every child, but it will be a favorite with those who love birds, the sea, or well-wrought prose. The nine brief chapters can be read aloud in one and a half to two hours.

Suggested Listening Level: Grades 4–8

Hans Andersen: His Classic Fairy Tales. TRANS- LATED BY ERIK HAUGAARD. *Illustrated by Michael Foreman.*   New York: Doubleday & Company, 1978.

Hans Christian Andersen's tales have been loved by American children ever since their first translation into English. The best translation available today is by Erik Haugaard, a Dane by birth who has lived in English-speaking countries most of his life and has written fine children's books of his own in English. This volume is a sensitive selection of seventeen of the best tales. It includes the one indispensable tale, "The Ugly Duckling," that every child deserves to hear in its complete and deeply touching form. (Everyone knows the story but often in a watered-down abridg- ment or a simplified cartoon version.) "The Wild Swans" and "The Tinderbox" are examples of traditional Danish fairy tales retold by Andersen. In "The Swineherd," "The Nightingale," and "The Dung Beetle," we find Andersen poking fun at the foibles of society. Perhaps the most original gift of Andersen, his ability to endow inanimate objects with life and emotions, is displayed in "The Darning Needle" and "The Steadfast Tin Soldier."

Two cautions: Most of Andersen's stories are not intended for or suited to little children. Both the romantic suffering of some tales and the tongue-in-cheek satire of others can be best appreciated by children of eight and up. "The Red Shoes," "The Snow Queen," and "The Little Match Girl" are extremely poignant at times—some would say excessively so—and have been known to haunt sensitive listeners. We recommend reading these yourself before deciding whether to share them with an audience of children.

Suggested Listening Level: Grades 3–8

Harriet Tubman, Conductor on the Underground Railroad BY ANNE PETRY. New York: Thomas Y. Crowell Company, 1955. Paperback: Pocket Books, Archway Paperbacks, 1971.

Ann Petry has written a first-rate biography about Harriet Tubman, who courageously made her way from slavery to freedom and then chose to make dangerous trips back to Tidewater Maryland to bring North more than three hundred other men, women, and children. Petry's eloquent prose creates a vivid picture of a slaveholding society, of the operation of the Underground Railroad, and of this remarkable woman. The first chapters set the scene; then the events of Harriet Tubman's life, narrated without exaggeration, build suspense and power. The last few pages are inevitably anticlimactic, for they describe the last, somewhat ordinary years of Tubman's life, but this merely sets off the amazing accomplishments of her earlier years.

Each chapter ends with an italicized passage of historical information, helping the listener to relate developments in Harriet's life to the events leading up to the Civil War, and introducing figures that were to play a part in national events or in Harriet's later life. As you read, try to indicate to your listeners the shift from the biographical narrative to this informative material. A few words or perhaps just a slight shift in tone will accomplish this. The book consists of twenty-two chapters of about eleven pages each, and total reading time is estimated at about five hours.

Suggested Listening Level: Grades 4–8

Henry Reed, Inc.   BY KEITH ROBERTSON.   *Illustrated by Robert McCloskey.*   New York: The Viking Press, 1958.   Paperback: Dell, 1974.

Faced with a summer in Princeton, New Jersey, and an assignment to make notes on "how things are at home" for his teacher at the American School in Naples, Italy, Henry Harris Reed decides to test the possibilities of the free-enterprise system. Working with the aid of neighbor Midge Glass, Henry comes to revise his opinion of females as well as test the endurance of his aunt and uncle, the neighbors, and "the System" itself. His efforts are earnest, logical, usually successful, and always involve at least one bit of outrageous slapstick comedy.

Henry is a serious straight man, a foil for Midge's more imaginative approach to problems. Henry occasionally delivers a rather long-winded digression that some readers may be tempted to condense or skip, but usually he gets an A-plus from listeners. When you finish the book, children may want to go on to read the sequels independently.

Suggested Listening Level: Grades 5–7

Hobberdy Dick BY KATHERINE BRIGGS. New York: Greenwillow Books, 1977.

A hobgoblin of the finest sort, Hobberdy Dick is dismayed to find there are new tenants for Wedford Manor, a Puritan city merchant and his family. Dick has guarded the Manor for the Culver family "for time out of mind," but the middle of the seventeenth century is not a happy time for hobgoblins or for those who believe in them. Before the story is over, however, Hobberdy Dick has helped Anne Sekar, the impoverished cousin of the old Culver family, and Joel Widdison, the merchant's son, find a treasure and save the fortunes of family and manor alike.

The setting of Puritan England is enhanced by Briggs's thorough understanding of hobgoblins and their lore. This is a story for romantics—those who know they are or wish they were. There is some awkward country dialect, especially in the conversations of the countryfolk and the hobgoblins. But none of them are around today, so plunge on with courage.

There are also some descriptive passages that it may be wise to skip, but these will differ with each reader and audience. The twenty-five chapters average approximately twenty minutes in reading time.

Suggested Listening Level: Grades 4–8

The Hobbit or There and Back Again   (revised edition) BY J.R.R. TOLKIEN. New York: Houghton Mifflin Company, 1937, 1938, and 1966. Paperback: Ballantine Books, 1965.

> In a hole in the ground there lived a hobbit. Not a nasty, dirty, wet hole, filled with ends of worms and an oozy smell, nor yet a dry, bare, sandy hole with nothing in it to sit down on or to eat: it was a hobbit-hole, and that means comfort.

Bilbo Baggins is the contented inhabitant of this hobbit-hole. Though Bilbo is devoted to his dinner and domestic comforts, as a hobbit should be, when Gandalf the wizard comes by one morning, Bilbo soon finds himself willy-nilly part of a remarkable adventure. He journeys through great perils with thirteen dwarves to try to recover a vast treasure from the dragon Smaug, and in the process proves that with determination and a stout heart, a rather ordinary being can rise to a heroic occasion.

Tolkien was a professor of Anglo-Saxon at Oxford University and drew on his wide knowledge of British folklore to create a believable world of dwarves, dragons, elves, and orcs. Names that enchant and deftly characterize, an undercurrent of humor, frequent sound effects, and rolling cadences add to the pleasure of reading this fantasy aloud. Each of the nineteen chapters is packed full of action, making this a book that provides reading for several weeks.

Suggested Listening Level: Grades 4–8

The House of Wings BY BETSY BYARS. *Illustrated by Daniel Schwartz.* New York: The Viking Press, 1972. Paperback: Penguin, Puffin Books, 1982.

Ten-year-old Sammy's parents, on their way from Alabama to Detroit in search of work, have left him with the grandfather he's never known while they go on to find a job and get settled. The boy, enraged at being abandoned, hates this strange old man who lives in a run-down house with a parrot, an owl, and a flock of geese who wander in and out, and the story opens with Sammy's desperate flight through strange countryside with his grandfather in pursuit.

In the midst of the chase, Sammy and his grandfather come upon a wounded crane, and gradually Sammy forgets his hurt and rage in the anxiety they share about the crane's fate. Byars is noted for her portraits of old people and for her ability to delicately depict the bond that many children feel with wild creatures—both gifts contribute to this touching, suspenseful book. The story has its funny moments, too, as Sammy learns how to coexist with the various feathered creatures his grandfather has taken in.

Because the action takes only twenty-four hours, and because it builds to a moving moment of understanding, *The House of Wings* has the gripping intensity of a classic short story. Sammy's life and his

grandfather's have been enriched by their first day together. So have ours.

The first of the fourteen chapters is fifteen pages
long; most are seven or eight pages and can be read
in about eight minutes each. *The Eighteenth Emer-
gency, The Midnight Fox, After the Goat Man, The
Cartoonist,* and *The Night Swimmers* are other books
by Betsy Byars that are successful read-alouds.

Suggested Listening Level: Grades 3–7

The House with a Clock in Its Walls BY JOHN
BELLAIRS. *Illustrated by Edward Gorey.*   New York:
The Dial Press, 1973. Paperback: Dell, 1974.

The year is 1948. Lewis Barnavelt, a recent orphan,
is traveling to his new home and an uncle he's never
met. That seems a fairly standard opening for a children's book, but from this point on a zany orginality
defeats all conventional expectations. Lewis's new
home turns out to be a huge, wonderful, and scary
Victorian mansion with a mysterious ticking in its
walls. Uncle Jonathan welcomes Lewis warmly, but he
and his neighbor and cook, Mrs. Zimmerman, engage
in all sorts of strange and secretive behavior—and unconventional language. "Weird Beard," "Frumpy,"
"Brush Mush," and "Hag Face" are only a few of the
epithets they affectionately hurl at each other.

Lewis discovers that this pair are a wizard and a
witch, and though they practice only benign magic,
they are pitted against the evil magic of the house's
previous owner. When Lewis himself dabbles in magic
to impress a friend, he sets off a chain of events lead-

ing to a calamity only he can prevent by finding and destroying the clock in the walls!

The eccentric characters, the paraphernalia of the occult, and the aura of mystery make this a good choice for preadolescents with a taste for the ghoulish. Nostalgic middle-aged readers, on the other hand, will enjoy such memorabilia as Super Suds radio commercials. Reading time is about four hours.

Suggested Listening Level: Grades 5–8

How to Eat Fried Worms BY THOMAS ROCKWELL. *Illustrated by Emily McCully.* New York: Franklin Watts, 1973. Paperback: Dell, 1975.

Billy had eaten a lot of things that most kids can't stand: fried liver, salmon loaf, mushrooms, tongue, and pig's feet. But could he really eat one worm a day for fifteen days? Alan and Joe bet that he couldn't. "Heck," said Billy, "I can gag *anything* down for fifty dollars!" Since Alan had to pay the fifty dollars out of accumulated savings, he and Joe try a number of schemes to sidetrack the determined Billy.

There are several debates here about just what's fair in a worm-eating contest. Are night crawlers really worms? (Yes.) Can the worms be chopped or minced? (No.) How *can* they be prepared? (Boiled, stewed, fried, or fricasseed—but all in one piece.) Are worms from a manure pile eligible? (No.) The details are just deliciously yucky enough to intrigue almost any group of young listeners. Total reading time is about an hour and a half, and we recommend breaks after the first, third, fourth, eighth, eleventh, and thirteenth worms for ten- to fifteen-minute sessions. It should be noted that a new librarian began her reading-aloud career with this book and gained a dubious kind of notoriety when one motivated sixth-grade listener brought worms to the school cafeteria and pretended to eat them. One of his friends threw up all over the lunch table, but even the vice-principal had to admit the story was funny.

Suggested Listening Level: Grades 3–6

The Hundred Penny Box   BY SHARON BELL MATHIS. *Illustrated by Leo and Diane Dillon.*   New York: The Viking Press, 1975.

Michael loves to count the pennies in his great-great-Aunt Dew's hundred penny box—one for every year of her life—while she shares with him her rich memories. But Michael's mother makes them both unhappy when she interrupts their game to make Aunt Dew take a nap. Worse, she wants to burn the hundred penny box because it's shabby and in the way. Only Michael understands how precious the box is to Aunt Dew, and he vows to save it.

This superb story doesn't gloss over the problems of old age: Aunt Dew's forgetfulness and her tactless ways; her monotonous singing of "Precious Lord, take my hand . . ."; the strains on the family that taking in an aged, infirm relative creates. Yet Aunt Dew's hundred-penny memories evoke a full life, and the empathy between the child and the old woman is drawn with rare skill. Leo and Diane Dillon's sepia-toned illustrations enhance the story's mood.

The contemplative mood of this quiet story can best be communicated in one reading session, which would require thirty to forty minutes.

Suggested Listening Level: Grades 3–6

The Incredible Journey BY SHEILA BURNFORD. Boston: Little, Brown and Company, 1961. Paperback: Bantam Books, 1981.

Three animals—a Siamese cat, an old English bull terrier, and a young golden retriever—lonesome for their old home and human family, set off on a journey of several hundred miles through the wilds of northwest Ontario. Their adventures will keep listeners on the edge of the chairs, but the suspense and danger alternate with touches of humor and warmth. The story is very convincing, true not only to dog and cat nature but to the characteristic behaviors of each breed. In addition, the distinctive and appealing personalities of each animal are quickly established, so that we share the author's obvious affection for them.

The Incredible Journey is an excellent choice for reading aloud to older reluctant readers. They will find the narrative very easy to follow and suspenseful, yet nothing in it suggests "a little kid's book." (As a matter of fact, it was published on the regular adult list and appeared for many weeks on the best-seller list when it came out.) Children as young as seven or eight will enjoy it too, so it would be a good family choice, especially when traveling.

There are eleven chapters. The first one painstakingly describes the region and the scene of comfort

and security that the animals will leave behind them.
Try to extend the first reading session to include
chapter two (this would require about thirty-five minutes total reading time), thus getting the animals on
their way before a break in the reading. If this is not
possible, ask your listeners to reserve judgment on the
story until after the second session.

Suggested Listening Level: Grades 3–8

The Iron Giant: A Story in Five Nights BY TED
HUGHES. *Drawings by Robert Nadler.* New York:
Harper & Row, 1968.

An Iron Giant, taller than a house, comes out of the
sea and feasts on the tractors, cars, and barbed-wire
fences of the nearby farms. A little boy named Hogarth
lures him into a deep pit and the farmers bury him.
But the Iron Giant digs his way out. Again the boy
has an idea. Why not supply the Giant with scrap
metal to feed on? It works and the Iron Giant lives
contentedly in a junkyard. Before the story ends, the
Iron Giant has saved the world from a terrible fate by
challenging and defeating a frightful monster from
outer space.

This strikingly original story is the work of a distinguished English poet, known for his vision of primitive power in the natural world. From a simple, repeti-
tive sentence-structure that would seem tedious in the
hands of most writers, Hughes manages to conjure an
epic dignity. The simplicity of syntax makes the book
accessible to poor readers, especially if they've listened
to it first. Here is a way to provide the young super-

hero fanatics you know with solid food for their imaginations. As the subtitle suggests, this story is best suited to five installments, one a day (or night) if possible.

Suggested Listening Level: Grades 2–5

Island of the Blue Dolphins BY SCOTT O'DELL. New York: Houghton Mifflin Company, 1960. Paperback: Dell, 1982.

This survival story, based on a historical event, has been enormously popular with children. The book chronicles the poignant life of Karana, an Indian girl born on an island off the California coast. When Russian and Aleut hunters come and kill many of the tribe, the Indians have no choice but to leave for the mainland. At the time of leaving, however, Karana discovers that her little brother is not on board the ship. She jumps overboard and is left behind with him.

The boy dies soon after this and Karana is alone in a harsh environment. She battles wild dogs, survives a tidal wave and earthquake, and attempts an unsuccessful journey in a dugout canoe to reach the mainland. The growth of her skills and her judgment, her painful wrestling with the taboos of her tribe (taboos that must be broken if she is to survive), and her eventual rescue after eighteen years make engrossing reading.

Narrated in a lucid, understated style, the book is an unflawed masterpiece. It is widely known to be a good book for reading aloud, though, so teachers should inquire in advance if children have already

heard it. The twenty-nine chapters are very short—
four or five pages in most cases.

Suggested Listening Level: Grades 4–6

Journey Outside BY MARY Q. STEELE. *Illustrated by
Rocco Negri.* New York: The Viking Press, 1969.
Paperback: Penguin, Puffin Books, 1979.

Journey Outside is an entirely original and beauti-
fully executed book. It is the story of Dilar, a young
member of the Raft People, who travel a dark underground river to the Better Place, fishing to supply
their needs. No one can tell Dilar where they are
going or where they have come from. All he can find
out is that his grandfather's grandfather had fond
memories of "day" and "green"—whatever they may be.

Dilar comes to suspect that his people are merely
traveling in an endless circle and, on an impulse, steps
from his raft to a ledge, letting the rafts go on without
him. To escape the vicious rats that close in on him,
Dilar claws his way up the rock walls, accidentally
finding his way to the world above ground. His gripping adventures in several very different societies have
the suspense of a good yarn and the provocativeness
of keen philosophical discussion, for Dilar is searching
to answer the eternal question: How should a person
live? Children from ten or eleven on are remarkably
responsive to such questions; *Journey Outside* will
stimulate much thought and discussion.

At the book's end, Dilar is searching for a way back
to the underground river so that he can show his
people "the light of day and the loveliness of green
growing things." Mrs. Steele's eloquent descriptions of

this world's marvels—the beauty of grass and trees, of birdsong and snowstorm—will help reader and listeners to experience them anew.

Suggested Listening Level: Grades 5–8

Julie of the Wolves BY JEAN CRAIGHEAD GEORGE. *Illustrated by John Schoenherr.* New York: Harper & Row, 1972. Paperback: Harper & Row, 1972.

Julie of the Wolves is a remarkable story of survival and of emotional and spiritual growth. Thirteen-year-old Miyax (Julie is her Americanized name) has been left parentless by her father's presumed death. Agreeing to an arranged marriage, she discovers that her husband is retarded, and she runs away when he tries to "mate" her. Before long she is lost on the vast North Slope of Alaska. Starving, she tries to recall the old lore that her father once shared with her, and manages to communicate her needs to a wolf pack. They bring her food, and with her primitive tools and knowledge of the old ways, she constructs a good life even as the Arctic winter closes in. The wolves become her family and the dream of reaching her pen pal in San Francisco, with which she started out, recedes. But the old ways are being eroded by encroaching technology; Amaroq, leader of the pack, is shot by hunters from an airplane. Julie discovers that her father is alive but has apparently given up the ancient values of his people. She must rethink her choices: it is clear that "the hour of the wolf and the eskimo is over."

Jean George's depiction of the fragile Arctic ecology is more persuasive than any lecture, yet smoothly inte-

grated with the plot. Children will be interested to
know that the wolf behavior depicted is based on research that Mrs. George studied and observed. She
obviously respects young people's ability to face the
difficult issues of our time and to handle complex and
challenging fiction.

The book has three parts. It is important for listeners
to realize that the second part is a flashback to the
circumstances of Miyax's life before she runs away.
(By the way, there is nothing explicit in the scene of
Daniel attempting to fulfill the role of husband, and it
should not be embarrassing to read or hear. The scene
cannot be skipped, for it explains why Julie leaves
home.)

My Side of the Mountain is another popular novel
by Jean George; she has written distinguished nonfiction for children as well.

Suggested Listening Level: Grades 6–8

Just So Stories   BY RUDYARD KIPLING.   1902.   Many
editions.

> Before the High and Far-Off Times, O my Best
> Beloved, came the Time of the Very Beginnings;
> and that was in the days when the Eldest Magi-
> cian was getting Things ready. First he got the
> Earth ready; then he got the Sea ready; and then
> he told all the Animals that they could come out
> and play.

Kipling's prose, larded with unusual and invented
words, flows with a rhythm and a rollicking sense of

language that set these stories as examples worth promoting in these days of diminishing articulateness. Each tale may be read independently and each is an explanation of the origin of something: how the camel got his hump, the rhinoceros his skin, the elephant his trunk. Two of them deal with the origin of the alphabet and of letter-writing, but the alphabet story is less appropriate for reading aloud because it relies on line drawings for clarification of the text.

These stories can be understood by children as young as five yet will be appreciated by older listeners, including adults. It should be noted, however, that Kipling was a Victorian gentleman and suffered from delusions of both male supremacy and white superiority. These assumptions are evident in many of the tales.

Suggested Listening Level: Grades 3–7

The Knee-High Man and Other Tales BY JULIUS LESTER. *Illustrated by Ralph Pinto.* New York: The Dial Press, 1972.

In the first of these trickster tales, Mr. Bear remarks that he doesn't know what trouble is. Mr. Rabbit, of course, obligingly sets right out to teach him. The book consists of six short tales based on American Black folklore. "Some are funny and some are sad," the author points out, but all are good stories.

The reading time is about five minutes for each tale, and they are suitable for any age group. Those who find the dialect of Joel Chandler Harris's Uncle Remus stories troublesome will be grateful to Mr.

Lester for making more accessible these tales about Mr. Rabbit, one of folklore's liveliest characters.

Suggested Listening Level: Grades K–5

The Lemming Condition   BY ALAN ARKIN.   *Illustrated by Joan Sandin.*   New York: Harper & Row, 1976. Paperback: Bantam Books, 1977.

All around Bubber his fellow lemmings are bustling about in excitement preparing to go west. Bubber expects to go, too, until his friend Crow reminds him of the ocean that lies at the foot of the cliffs to the west and asks if lemmings can swim. Once Bubber begins to question the wisdom of the mass suicide that is the lemming condition, he becomes an outsider. Instead of the acceptance and feeling of solidarity shared by all the other lemmings, Bubber is full of anxiety and despair. When the lemmings begin running, Bubber is swept along. Only at the last moment does he find the strength to resist.

Alan Arkin, distinguished actor and director, is a talented writer as well. His ability to develop character and plot with no words wasted gives this little book considerable impact. Children will like the comical interchanges between Bubber and the other sharply drawn characters, but will be receptive as well to the underlying parable. The book's six chapters can be read aloud in approximately one hour.

Suggested Listening Level: Grades 4–8

The Light Princess   BY GEORGE MACDONALD.   *Illustrated by Maurice Sendak.*   New York: Farrar, Straus & Giroux, 1977.

Imagine losing your gravity—being not only light-bodied but light-minded! A princess who floats out of the hands of nursemaids, tutors, and parents is bad enough, but one who laughs immoderately when the enemy threatens her father's city is intolerable. The king and queen know she has been enchanted by the king's sister, the Princess Makemnoit, and they discover that only in the water of the nearby lake does the princess have any real freedom. Philosophers Hum-Drum and Kopy-Keck finally decide that if external water is efficacious, then "water from a deeper source might work a perfect cure; in short, that if the poor afflicted princess could by any means be made to cry, she might recover her lost gravity."

Enchantments, a giggling princess, a fine, fair prince, pompous philosophers—these elements of traditional lore have been whipped into an elegant froth of a tale for sophisticated listeners. MacDonald's touches of farce offer an experienced reader opportunity to rant and rave as the Princess Makemnoit (sour, spiteful creature that she is); to wave a finger portentously as a metaphysical philosopher; or to giggle with the heroine, the de*light*ful princess.

Sendak's drawings are dolefully droll and should be shared with an audience after each reading. The book can be read two or three chapters at a time and completed in less than two hours.

Suggested Listening Level: Grades 4–8

The Lion, the Witch and the Wardrobe BY C. S. LEWIS. *Illustrated by Pauline Baynes.* New York: Macmillan, 1951. Paperback: Macmillan, 1970.

Four children have been evacuated during the London blitz to the huge old country house of an elderly professor. During a rainy-day indoor game of hide-and-seek, the youngest, Lucy, shuts herself in a large wardrobe among the fur coats. Discovering that the wardrobe has no back wall, she makes her way deeper into it and finds herself in Narnia, an unhappy land where, thanks to the evil White Witch, it is "always winter and never Christmas." With much difficulty, Lucy persuades her older siblings of the existence of Narnia and of the part they are destined to play in the restoration of the true ruler of Narnia, Aslan the Lion.

The realistic interaction among the four children is as skillfully drawn as the fantastic Talking Animals, fauns, and giants who people Narnia. Together they make this and its sequels one of the best-loved fantasies in all of children's literature.

Lewis intended *The Chronicles of Narnia* as Christian allegory, but children of all faiths respond to the compelling events and images on their own terms. The seventeen chapters each require about ten minutes' reading time.

Suggested Listening Level: Grades 3–8

The Little Bookroom BY ELEANOR FARJEON. *Illustrated by Edward Ardizzone.* New York: Henry Z. Walck, 1956; Oxford University Press, 1979.

Eleanor Farjeon's world has been called by J. S. Beresford "a world of sunlight, of gay inconsequence, of emotional surprise, a world of poetry, delight, and humor." Although in her long and productive career she wrote poems, plays, and retellings of legends and saints' lives, among other things, this world has survived most vividly in her stories. *The Little Bookroom* is a generous selection of those stories, compiled by Eleanor Farjeon herself at the age of seventy-three. If you have a taste for the whimsical, the romantic, and the linguistically playful, you will find tales here to captivate you. Many of them, such as our favorite, "The Seventh Princess," take the familiar conventions of fairy tales and set them charmingly on their heads. Whether they take place in a neverland ("Westwoods," for instance) or our own world ("San Fairy Ann" and "Pennyworth"), the stories are full of dazzling invention and daring coincidence.

Because they are cake and not bread, so to speak, the tales are best enjoyed in small helpings. We suggest you read only one or two at a time. Some of the stories are as short as three pages; others are quite long and require forty minutes or so to read aloud.

Suggested Listening Level: Grades 3–5

Little House in the Big Woods BY LAURA INGALLS WILDER. *Illustrated by Garth Williams.* New York: Harper & Brothers, 1953. Paperback: Harper & Row, 1973.

Many a family now grown up looks back on the reading aloud of the "Little House" books as a treasured memory of family life. The eight books in the series* are a skillfully fictionalized account of Mrs.

---

* A ninth volume, *The First Four Years,* has been marketed with the series, but it was published from a manuscript

Wilder's childhood in a pioneering family that moved from one place to another, struggling to survive in a lovely yet often inhospitable wilderness. Each scene and event is shown through the eyes of Laura, a wonderfully lively and sensitive heroine. Mrs. Wilder was in her sixties when she began writing books, and it is remarkable how convincingly she was able to capture the perceptions of a young child. In *Little House in the Big Woods,* the first book, Laura is four and five years old; later books record her growing up, ending with marriage at eighteen to Almanzo Wilder. (*Farmer Boy* is not about the Ingalls family, but describes Almanzo's childhood on a prosperous farm in upstate New York.)

To the adult, the books are a fascinating chronicle of nineteenth-century child-rearing, a critique of the doctrine of Manifest Destiny (especially *Little House on the Prairie*), and a tribute to the courage and endurance of the western pioneers. To the child, they are exciting adventure stories and sensitive renderings of childhood experiences. Children are fascinated by how different Laura's life is from their own: Laura encounters a bear in the cow pen, Indians on the warpath, and a plague of locusts. Furthermore, she is ecstatic when Santa brings her a tin cup of her own and a whole penny! Yet today's children find Laura

---

found after Mrs. Wilder's death. She did not intend it as part of the series, probably because it chronicled an unremitting series of disasters in the early years of the Wilder marriage, and it does not read well aloud.

just like themselves in many ways—they have experienced her feelings of mixed delight and terror when her daddy plays at being a "mad dog," and her fierce jealousy of sister Mary's blond hair.

The books are now established classics of children's literature and are part of the library heritage of every American. Though they depict a somewhat idealized family, they are much less sentimental and more original than the television series that has been loosely— very loosely—based on them. *Little House in the Big Woods* consists of thirteen short chapters. The sequels become gradually longer and more complex in style, as they in effect grow up with Laura.

Suggested Listening Level: Grades K–3

The Loner BY ESTER WIER. *Illustrated by Christine Price.* New York: David McKay Co., 1963.

This is a story of a boy who was so alone that he didn't even have a name. He traveled with a group of migrant workers until the day that his only friend was killed in a threshing accident. Full of grief, the boy decides that he will go to California but wanders alone until a woman sheepherder known as Boss finds him on the Montana prairie and takes him in. These two lonely, independent people are suspicious of each other, but slowly come to an understanding. The boy learns to read and picks the name of David, the shepherd king of the Bible. He longs to live up to the strength of the biblical David but makes mistakes with the sheep; learning to be responsible is hard work. It is David, however, who finds and kills the grizzly that had attacked Boss's son, and both woman and boy realize that being lonely is not the same as being alone. They share a faith in themselves and in each other.

This is a stark story, described in spare prose, but Wier involves the reader/listener in David's plight from the first page. David and Boss are introspective characters, however, and this may slow the story down for some listeners. The chapters are relatively short and can be combined to form perhaps four or five sessions.

Suggested Listening Level: Grades 5–7

M. C. Higgins, the Great BY VIRGINIA HAMILTON. New York: Macmillan, 1974. Paperback: Dell, 1980.

M. C. Higgins sits on top of his pole, high above the treetops where he can see all over the mountain— Sarah's Mountain, named for his great-grandmother who came here long ago fleeing slavery. He sees the thick woods and the lake and, above his family's home, the ugly spoil-heap of the strip mine.

M.C. is a black boy fast growing to manhood and all that it entails. For one thing, he can't stop thinking about the city girl who is camping by the lake. For another, he finds himself in combat with the father he loves, not only in their fierce wrestling, but in other ways. Jones Higgins forbids his son to associate with Ben Killburn or any of his "witchy" family. But M.C. cannot give up his friend. Even more serious is their disagreement over the spoil heap. M.C. believes it will slide down and kill them all; he tries to persuade his father that they must leave. But Jones's mind is closed. Sarah's Mountain is their place.

M.C. then works out his own plan. He'll bring home the dude who has been traveling over the mountains recording singers' voices. When he hears M.C.'s mother sing, he'll make a star out of her and they'll have enough money to move. Nothing works out quite as M.C. wants, but he comes to understand that the family's heritage binds them to the mountain. And Jones, overcoming old superstitions, accepts Ben.

Those who want the meaning of every act and image in a book to be crystal-clear may find Virginia Hamilton's work difficult. Symbols and images that cannot be readily explicated are central to her vision of life. The meaning of the work emerges gradually. Encourage your listeners to approach the book as they would poetry and they will find it a powerful experience.

The book's fourteen chapters are long, averaging about thirty minutes each when read aloud.

Suggested Listening Level: Grades 7–8

Many Moons BY JAMES THURBER. *Illustrated by Louis Slobodkin.* New York: Harcourt Brace and World, 1943. Paperback: Harcourt Brace Jovanovich, 1978.

"Anything your heart desires" is what the King promises his daughter, the Princess Lenore. "I want the moon," she says. So the King asks, in turn, the Lord High Chamberlain, the Royal Wizard, and the Royal Mathematician, but although they produce prodigious lists ranging from ambergris to wolfbane, none can get the moon. It is the Court Jester who suggests that the Princess Lenore be consulted about the size and distance of the moon, and it is the Court

Jester and Princess Lenore—and the moon—who solve the problem of one moon too many.

Many of Thurber's writings make good reading aloud, from the hilarity of allegedly autobiographical essays like "The Night the Bed Fell" and "University Days" in *My Life and Hard Times* to the mock fairy tale of *The Thirteen Clocks*, with its tongue-tangling witticisms. *Many Moons,* however, is so good for a wide audience range, for a one-session book, and for its very matter-of-fact, no-nonsense princess that it just had to be included. The story stands on its own, although Slobodkin's illustrations give it the appearance of a picture book. The beginning reader will want to practice this a bit, as the lists produced by the Royal Consultants need to flow "trippingly" off the tongue. It is not difficult, however, and can be enjoyed by primary grades through fourth or fifth in one twenty-minute session.

Suggested Listening Level: Grades K–4

Mary Poppins   BY PAMELA L. TRAVERS. *Illustrated by Mary Shepard.* New York: Harcourt Brace & World, 1934, 1962; revised edition, 1981.   Paperback: Harcourt Brace Jovanovich, 1972; revised edition, 1981.

Most children know Mary Poppins from the well-loved film. But they should be introduced to the sharp-tongued, strait-laced Mary Poppins of Pamela Travers's book, for she possesses some special magic that no film-maker has yet captured. Some children may resist, feeling they know "the best parts" from the movie. Do insist. The conversations between the babies and the "cheeky Starling," for instance, or the Dancing Cow's story—told in her own words—are too good to miss.

We would suggest, however, that the reader who is using the original edition omit the chapter "Bad Tuesday." There is no plot element here on which future action depends, and the stereotyped roles assigned to the characters from the four corners of the world are offensive to all. Fortunately, in the revised edition this chapter has been rewritten to eliminate the objectionable stereotyping.

The book can be read in about three hours. They will be three hours well spent, for Mary Poppins is one of those rare characters in literature who remains unforgettable . . . no matter which way the wind blows.

Suggested Listening Level: Grades 2–4

Mister Corbett's Ghost BY LEON GARFIELD. *Illustrated by Alan Cober.* New York: Pantheon Books, 1968.

Garfield has written a gripping tale of a mistreated apothecary's apprentice, whose hatred for his harsh master apparently causes the master's sudden death. Saddled first with the corpse and then with the ghost of his nemesis, however, young Ben soon comes to regret his impulsive action. Garfield is a master at creating atmosphere, and his vividly evoked gloom of a bitter New Year's Eve in eighteenth-century London is reminiscent of Dickens's *A Christmas Carol*, as is the very touching reconciliation at the book's end.

Corbett's rich and vigorous prose style makes his fiction ideal for oral reading. The story is a good choice for upper elementary and middle school children with their notorious ghoulish taste, yet the tale is a deeply moral one that will engage children's ethical imaginations.

Make sure before you begin that the children know what an apprentice is and how much apprentices used to be at the mercy of the master. It helps, too, to know that Highgate Hill and Hampstead Heath outside of London were the territory of highwaymen and outlaws. The tale is told in eight short chapters, which could be read two at a time over four brief sessions.

Suggested Listening Level: Grades 5–8

Mr. Popper's Penguins BY RICHARD AND FLORENCE ATWATER. *Illustrated by Robert Lawson.* Boston: Little, Brown and Company, 1938. Paperback: Dell, 1980.

Mr. Popper was a dreamer. A rather untidy, forgetful house painter, he was destined to become the most famous person in Stillwater, for Mr. Popper dreamed of faraway places like the Antarctic. Because of his interest in an expedition to the South Pole, Mr. Popper and his family receive a penguin named Captain Cook. They find, however, that penguins are social creatures—and Captain Cook is lonely. So Greta arrives to keep the Captain company and eventually the Popper family expands to include twelve sociable penguins.

The ordinary, even prosaic, qualities of the Popper family and their town of Stillwater are wonderful contrasts to Mr. Popper's acceptance of the penguins and their antics. The chapters are short enough to be read in five or ten minutes if a group gets wiggly, but a twenty-minute session will hold most listeners. This story with Robert Lawson's drawings is a surefire choice for primary grades, especially second- and third-graders, or as a first longer story for kindergarten or first grade.

Suggested Listening Level: Grades K–3

Misty of Chincoteague BY MARGUERITE HENRY. *Illustrated by Wesley Dennis.* Chicago: Rand McNally & Company, 1947. Paperback: Rand McNally & Company, 1947.

"Legends be the only stories as is true!" explains Grandpa Beebe to Maureen and Paul. Some on Chincoteague Island would say it was only a legend that the wild horses on nearby Assateague were descendants of a stallion and his mares from a Spanish ship that went down in a gale. The two children care less about legends than the horses themselves, in particular a mare named Phantom. At the annual Pony Penning Day, they use hard-earned savings to buy Phantom and her new silver and gold colt, Misty. Phantom, "like a piece of thistledown borne by the wind, moving through space with wild abandon," wins the race with Black Comet. Later Phantom is lured back to the wild freedom of Assateague by the stallion the Pied Piper, but by then Misty is old enough to live with the children and their grandparents quite happily as the center of attention.

The story of Phantom and Misty, as well as the stories of Misty's offspring *Sea Star* and *Stormy,* revolve around the traditional Pony Penning Days on the two islands off the Virginia coast. A good story for middle grade animal-lovers, *Misty of Chincoteague* divides into about nine twenty-minute sessions.

Suggested Listening Level: Grades 3–5

Mrs. Frisby and the Rats of NIMH   BY ROBERT C. O'BRIEN.   *Illustrated by Zena Bernstein.*   New York: Atheneum, 1971.   Paperback: Atheneum, 1971.

Mrs. Frisby is at her wit's end. The fieldmouse widow and mother has a sick son and needs help in moving him out of the way of spring planting. As a last resort she consults the rats under the rose bush and finds there an unexpectedly sophisticated civilization. It turns out that the rats and Mr. Frisby had been part of an experimental group at the National Institute of Mental Health (NIMH), and the series of injections that they got not only enhanced their mental abilities but prolonged their life-span.

"By teaching us how to read, they taught us how to get away," explains Nicodemus, leader of the rats of NIMH, to Mrs. Frisby. Now, five years after they escaped from NIMH, the group is working on the Plan, a long-range scheme for survival that won't involve stealing as a way of life.

Mrs. Frisby's own courage and initiative are supplemented by the rats' help, and her problem is resolved. The success of the rats' noble experiment is still in doubt, however, when the book ends. Thought-provoking and engrossing, the story is just plausible enough to spark stimulating discussions by fifth- and sixth-grade listeners. This surefire novel is also suitable for a wide age-range of listeners because it operates on many levels, and the twenty-eight chapters combine into approximately fourteen twenty-minute sessions.

Suggested Listening Level: Grades 4–7

The Moffats BY ELEANOR ESTES. *Illustrated by Louis Slobodkin.* New York: Harcourt Brace and World, 1941. Paperback: Harcourt Brace Jovanovich, 1968.

The Moffats was published over forty years ago, and it had a backward-looking "olden days" charm about it even then. This is small-town America in the days of horse-drawn wagons and coalyards, but children today will discover that they have much in common with the four Moffat children. All the joys and worries of childhood are deftly captured: Joe's despair when he discovers he has lost the money Mama gave him for coal; the children's terror at the ghost that they set up themselves to scare the boastful Peter Frost; and Jane's relief at discovering that the Chief of Police isn't looking for reasons to arrest a little girl—he's even nice! The fatherless family is poor and can scarcely eke out an existence on Mama's dressmaking money until the next customer pays her, but humor and a sense of loving security predominate, which makes it a good choice for the primary grades.

Each chapter is a complete and satisfying episode—twelve in all. There are two other Moffat books, for those who have enjoyed this one: *Rufus M*. and *The Middle Moffat. Ginger Pye* is another of Estes' books that is still popular with children. In *The Hundred*

Dresses, Estes strikes a more serious note; it captures the misery a group of children can inflict on a child who is different.

Suggested Listening Level: Grades 1–4

Moon Eyes   BY JOSEPHINE POOLE.   *Illustrated by Trina Schart Hyman.*   Boston: Atlantic–Little, Brown, 1967.

"First we'll wait, then we'll whistle, then we'll dance together." Those are the words Kate sees written around the statue in the garden pond shortly after her father goes off to recover from her mother's death. Later a looming black dog with silvery gray-white eyes appears in the garden. And when the tall, angular but "arresting" Rhoda Cantrip turns up, a bewitched Kate finds herself inviting the woman to be a guest in the house. Soon Kate's mute younger brother, Thomas, seems to be the focus of gathering evil power as Rhoda Cantrip begins to dominate the household. The housekeeper, Mrs. Beers, warns Kate about witches and their spells, but Kate feels she must wage war with Rhoda or risk losing Thomas and the house to the evil represented by the strange woman and her dog, Moon Eyes.

Although the story unfolds rather slowly in the first two chapters, both reader and listeners are soon caught in the web of events that threaten Kate and young Thomas. Some plot elements may not bear the light of logic, but then, witches' charms are more potent when their weaving is slightly murky. The book appeals to older listeners with an interest in the occult.

Suggested Listening Level: Grades 6–8

The Mouse and His Child BY RUSSELL HOBAN. *Illustrated by Lillian Hoban.* New York: Harper & Row, 1967. Paperback: Hearst, Avon Books, 1974.

On a toy-store counter a clockwork mouse turns around and around, swinging his child up and down by the arms as he circles. The mouse-child wants to stay forever in the cozy store, but "one does what one is wound to do"; their fate as toys is to be bought and go out into the world. They are soon broken and discarded, but a tramp repairs them, winds them, and sets them down in the road. "Be tramps," he says, and walks away.

The journey that follows, like most odysseys, is a search for a place in the world and for family. Listeners will be as caught up in the fate of these tin figures and the animals they meet as in the most realistic adventure story. At the same time, the encounters of the mouse and his child with ruthless rat criminals, forest mob violence, and a senseless war between bands of shrews will be thought-provoking for listeners of all ages. Don't expect the gentle and endearing mood of many toy fantasies. Much of this one is closer to Orwell's *Animal Farm* than to *Winnie-the-Pooh*. But the perils do give way to justice and contentment at the end.

Russell Hoban has written classic picture books (such as *Bedtime for Frances*) and highly acclaimed novels for adults (*Riddley Walker*, for instance). He pays children the compliment of using some challenging words and disturbing ideas in this book. We especially recommend it for gifted children and for young adolescents beginning to question the ways of the world. The book is divided into ten episodic chapters.

Suggested Listening Level: Grades 4–8

Mouse Woman and the Vanished Princesses BY CHRISTIE HARRIS. *Illustrated by Douglas Tait.* New York: Atheneum, 1976.

". . . In the days of very long ago, when things were different," narnauks, or supernatural beings, mingled with the native tribes of the Pacific northwest. Often, assuming the guise of a handsome young man, a narnauk would entice a princess away from the safety of the totem-pole village into the spirit world. This was a great tribal calamity, for the princesses carried the royal bloodlines. One narnauk disapproved of all this and made it her business to advise and aid the captive princesses. This was Mouse Woman—sometimes a tiny, busy, large-eyed woman, sometimes a daring mouse—but always "a very, very proper little person."

Though each of the six stories in this collection concerns Mouse Woman's rescue of a princess, they vary a good deal. "The Princess and the Feathers" tells of a courageous princess who escapes a horrible death, thanks to her quick wits and Mouse Woman's help. The princess of "The Princess and the Bears," on the other hand, is spoiled and petulant. Her marriage to the Prince-of-Bears is the narnauk's way of ensuring peace and respect between her tribe and the bears. "The Princess and the Geese" is a romantic tale reminiscent of Celtic tales about the selchies, or seal people. "The Princess and the Magic Plume" is a gruesome story; we found it less appealing than the others but know middle school students who would probably relish it.

In the course of skillfully retelling these old legends, Christie Harris conveys a clear picture of an ancient way of life and of the values that underlie it. Older children will be interested in the similarities and differences between them and European folktales. The stories vary in length, but most can be read in one sitting.

Suggested Listening Level: Grades 4–8

The Mousewife BY RUMER GODDEN.   *Illustrated by Heidi Holder.*   New York: The Viking Press, 1982.

Once a little mousewife befriended a dove caged in Miss Barbara Wilkinson's parlor. Whenever she could snatch a moment from her nest-making and crumb-collecting, she visited the dejected bird. From him, she learned about flying free above the treetops and how the wind made different patterns in cornfields and how dew tasted in the early morning. She finally realized that the dove needed to be out in the world, so one night she released the lock and he escaped through an open window. The mousewife sadly wonders who will tell her now about the great world outside. But then she sees the stars. . . .

This quiet, gentle story catches the essence of a master writer as the mousewife shares the dreams of the dove to soar beyond a cage, to know the stars. So many of this author's works are successful when read aloud—from her doll stories like *Impunity Jane* to the novel *Episode of Sparrows*—but somehow this "different" mousewife is most memorable. The story can be read in one sitting.

Suggested Listening Level: Grades 2–7

My Father's Dragon BY RUTH STILES GANNETT. *Illustrated by Ruth Chrisman Gannett.* New York: Random House, 1948. Paperback: Dell, 1980.

Does your father tell tall tales? One father told his child about his rescue of a dragon from Wild Island where lazy animals kept it prisoner. It seems that the dragon (a baby about the size of a large bear, with a long tail, yellow and blue stripes, gold wings, and bright red eyes and horn) was required to fly those lazy animals across the river that nearly split Wild Island in two. So the child's father set off to befuddle the lazy animals, rescue that baby dragon, and fly away home.

Stuff and nonsense? Of course, but it is so absurd and so full of colorful detail that younger audiences are captured just as surely as the baby dragon was. We have found that tall tales are sometimes over the heads of children under eight or nine, but images of a lion with seven different-colored hair ribbons in his mane (because his mother hates messy manes) or seventeen crocodiles tail-to-tail as a bridge across the river, or tigers chewing gum until it turns green enough to plant, are vivid enough to convince even younger listeners that this is funny. The ten chapters can be read in about an hour and a half, and the adventures of the dragon and the narrator's father continue in *The Dragons of Blueland*.

Suggested Listening Level: Grades K–4

Oliver Hyde's Dishcloth Concert BY RICHARD KEN-
NEDY. *Illustrated by Robert Andrew Parker.* Boston:
Atlantic–Little, Brown, 1977.

Oliver Hyde lived alone, full of grief and bitterness.
Sometimes the children from town sang a taunting
little rhyme:

> The beautiful bride of Oliver Hyde,
> Fell down dead on the mountainside.

And ever since his bride's death, Oliver Hyde "sat
cold, dark, and quiet on his little hill." One day an
old friend came to ask Oliver Hyde to play the fiddle
for little Sue's wedding—Oliver having played the
sweetest fiddle in the country. But he said he wouldn't
come unless folks would wear a dishcloth on their
heads, and Oliver was sure no one would agree. When
the wedding day came, however, Oliver Hyde was
surprised to learn how much better it is to fiddle for
other people than to be miserable by yourself.

Don't let the format of this cadenced tale fool
you into thinking of it only for primary grades.
Third- through fifth-grade listeners are also an appropriate audience for this twenty-minute story. It
seems natural to put it with a bit of music, fiddle or
otherwise, and to let listeners try it on their own to
enjoy Parker's illustrations.

Suggested Listening Level: Grades 3–5

Orphans of the Wind   BY ERIK CHRISTIAN HAUGAARD.
Illustrated by Milton Johnson. Boston: Houghton
Mifflin Company, 1966.

Jim, a twelve-year-old orphan, is virtually sold by his
tightfisted, coldhearted uncle into service as a deck
boy on a brig sailing out of Bristol. At sea, the crew
learn that they sail not for Boston but for Charleston
with an illegal cargo of guns and powder for the Con-
federacy. Jim listens to the men argue slavery and the
rights and wrongs of the war, struggling to work out
what he believes. His own bitter subjection to his
uncle brings him to appreciate the evil of human
bondage, and he joins those who oppose the ship's
mission. Before they can act, the ship burns off the
Carolina coast. Jim and the three sailors he has come
to care for most make their way to shore in a damaged
boat and then travel north to join the Union Army. At
the Battle of Bull Run, Jim learns first-hand of the
confusion and waste of war.

As in his other fine historical novels, Erik Haugaard
spins an enthralling yarn while he challenges his
young audience to understand the human choices that
shaped people's lives in the past. Attentive young
listeners will recognize that similar choices confront
them today. Allow four to five hours' total reading
time for the nineteen chapters and epilogue.

Suggested Listening Level: Grades 5–8

The Other World: Myths of the Celts   BY MARGARET
HODGES. *Illustrated by Eros Keith.* New York:
Farrar, Straus & Giroux, 1973 (out of print).

This collection of ten stories retold from Celtic folk-lore demonstrates why the Celts have been renowned as storytellers. Some of the tales are comical, some romantic; some ring with epic bravado, others are steeped in tragic foreboding. We recommend that for reading aloud you start with "The Lad of Luck and the Monster of the Loch," a rollicking folktale with more fantastic creatures—mermaids, giants, and monsters—per page than one would think possible. Another satisfying story, equally compelling and more romantic, is "Tam Lin." Burd Janet, a lass with a mind of her own, falls in love with Tam Lin, a handsome knight, and with great courage rescues him from the fairy queen's clutches at dark midnight on Halloween. A reading of "Tam Lin" would add to any Halloween observance for older children, though you needn't wait for that holiday. More challenging for both reader and listener are the retellings of the legends of the great Irish heroes, Cuchulain, Finn MacCool, and Dermot.

The last three selections in the book are stories from Arthurian legend. Mrs. Hodges has retained the wonder and power of these ancient stories without the stiff, archaic language of so many other versions. Older children with their sensitivity to issues of loyalty and treachery, courage and idealism, have loved these tales for generations. In our time, they often encounter the legends only on screen. These three tales, plus the bibliography that follows, can lead children to their rich literary origins.

Margaret Hodges has published sensitive retellings of myths from other cultures as well. Especially popu-

lar with children from third grade on is her version
of a Paiute Indian tale, *Fire Bringer*.

Suggested Listening Level: Grades 5–8

Over Sea, Under Stone   BY SUSAN COOPER.   *Illustrated
by Margery Gill.*   New York: Harcourt Brace Jovanovich, 1966.   Paperback: Harcourt Brace Jovanovich,
1979.

The Drew children, Simon, Jane, and Barney, discover an ancient manuscript in the attic of their summer home in Cornwall, and find themselves thereby
drawn into a life-and-death struggle. The narrative is
both a classic mystery story in which the children race
into and out of heart-stopping dangers as they try to
get the treasure before the bad guys do, and, on
another level, the lofty and perilous quest for the Grail
itself—King Arthur's legacy to the forces of light in
their eternal battle against the dark. The staunch figure of Great-uncle Merry, university professor and
world authority on Arthurian matters, plays an important part in guiding and occasionally rescuing the
children in their quest.

A few minor characters speak a Cornish dialect; we
recommend trying out a few of these lines in advance
to determine whether you want to attempt the accent
or ignore it. Susan Cooper has written four more books
that carry on the battle of the Light versus the Dark;
none of these is as firmly rooted in a realistic narrative
as this one, however. Written in the mode of "high
fantasy," they are increasingly dominated by the marvels of ancient folklore.

It should be noted that Jane is, in this first book, a

rather stereotyped female, very much in the shadow of her more heroic brothers. In the third volume of the series, *Greenwitch,* she takes the central role.

Suggested Listening Level: Grades 4–7

Owls in the Family BY FARLEY MOWAT. *Illustrated by Robert Frankenberg.* Boston: Atlantic–Little, Brown, 1961.

Billy already had a few pets when he approached his parents about keeping an owl blown out of its nest after a heavy windstorm. There were about thirty gophers snared on the Saskatchewan prairie with the help of Bruce and Murray, and rats from the medical school where Murray's father was a professor (no one was quite sure how many because they kept having babies so fast), a box of garter snakes under the back porch, and pigeons—about ten of them, but they kept bringing friends and relations for visits. And Mutt, of course, but he wasn't just a dog—he was family. So an owl didn't seem so overwhelming when one thought about it. Later, when Wol was joined by a timid, be-draggled second owl named Weeps, the menagerie was complete. But life with owls and rats and gophers and pigeons and snakes was not calm, and Billy had a difficult time keeping animals and humans separate and happy.

This first-person account based on the author's Canadian childhood is a perfect choice for third-through sixth-grade classes restless with the lure of spring and the itch to be outside. The episodic chapters are "knee-slappers" and the action is fast-paced, taking approximately two and a half hours' reading time. Slightly older children find Mowat's adventure novels, such as *Lost in the Barrens,* totally engrossing.

Suggested Listening Level: Grades 3–6

Ozma of Oz   BY L. FRANK BAUM.   *Illustrated by John R. Neill.*   Chicago: The Reilly and Lee Co., 1907. Paperback: Ballantine Books, 1979.

Why do we suggest *Ozma of Oz* rather than Baum's first and best-known book, *The Wizard of Oz?* Because nearly all American children are well-acquainted with the film version of *The Wizard of Oz* from its annual television screenings; because we, like most other critics, think that the film improves upon the book, which is therefore likely to prove a disappointment; and because we believe that Baum had not yet perfected his craft when he wrote *The Wizard of Oz. Ozma of Oz* seems to us a better book. In particular, it reads aloud better.

In this book children will find Dorothy reunited with her dear friends from Oz: the Scarecrow, the Tin Woodman, and the Cowardly Lion. And she has acquired amusing new friends—Billina, a talking hen of strong opinions and quick wits; Tiktok, a mechanical man who serves Dorothy devotedly; and the capable and gracious Ozma, girl ruler of Oz. From the storm at sea in chapter one that blows Dorothy and Billina overboard, to the successful rescue of the Queen of Ev and her ten children from the diabolically clever enchantments of the Nome King, the listener's interest never flags. Dorothy is as appealing as ever— open, brave, and self-assured. When a princess commands haughtily: "Tell me, . . . are you of royal blood?" our heroine replies, "Better than that, ma'am, . . . I came from Kansas."

Our only caution for readers-aloud is that Baum describes the mechanical man's words as "uttered all in the same tone, without any change of expression." Most listeners cannot make sense out of expressionless words, and besides, it is tiresome to read without inflection for long. We recommend therefore that you make Tiktok's speech only slightly mechanical.

Suggested Listening Level: Grades 2–5

The Peppermint Pig BY NINA BAWDEN. Philadelphia: J. B. Lippincott Company, 1975. Paperback: Penguin, Puffin Books, 1977.

Looking for an opening that will grab kids' attention? Try this one:

> Old Granny Greengrass had her finger chopped off in the butcher's when she was buying half a leg of lamb. She had pointed to the place where she wanted her joint to be cut but then she decided she needed a bigger piece and pointed again. Unfortunately, Mr. Grummett, the butcher, was already bringing his sharp chopper down. He chopped straight through her finger and it flew like a snapped twig into a pile of sawdust in the corner of the shop. It was hard to tell who was more surprised, Granny Greengrass, or the butcher. But she didn't blame him. She said, "I could never make up my mind and stick to it, Mr. Grummett, that's always been my trouble."

Poll, nine, and Theo, ten and a half, love to hear their mother tell this old family story. Big brother

George says they're partial to bloodthirsty stories because their own lives are so snug and comfortable. Before long, though, their comfortable life is behind them. Their father confesses to a theft he didn't commit, loses his job, and goes away to America to make his fortune. While he's gone, the rest of the family must leave London to live with their father's sisters in a Norfolk village. For Poll, it is a wonderful and terrible year. The best thing in it is Johnnie, a runt pig who becomes an adored pet with the run of the household. But the inevitable slaughter of Johnnie, and Poll's growing certainty that her father will never return, are a part of the year too. Poll, feisty and sensitive, makes this coming-of-age novel one that appeals to children and adults, boys and girls. The story is so universal that the few unfamiliar British words and phrases provide flavor without offering any real difficulty. The book consists of nine chapters, each about thirty minutes long.

Suggested Listening Level: Grades 4–8

The Phantom Tollbooth   BY NORTON JUSTER.   *Illustrated by Jules Feiffer.*   New York: Random House, 1961.   Paperback: Random House, 1961.

Milo is bored by everything until he discovers in his room a turnpike tollbooth, complete with a strange map. When he gamely sets out in his toy car, the tollbooth admits him to a strange land where the marvels and adventures quickly banish his boredom. In the cities of Dictionopolis and Digitopolis, Milo's dull school subjects take on new meaning, and he discovers that he has to think his way out of trouble. Idioms become literal as Milo meets a Spelling Bee, gets stuck in the Doldrums, visits the Land of Infinity ("a dreadfully poor place . . . they can never manage to make ends meet"), and attends a banquet where the speakers have to eat their words. Among the memorable characters he encounters are Faintly Macabre, the not-so-wicked witch, and Kakofonous A. Dischord, Doctor of Dissonance. Milo's adventures end happily as he restores peace to the land by rescuing the Princesses Rhyme and Reason from the Mountains of Ignorance.

Some children love this book's wordplay and intellectual gymnastics; others find it tedious in its absence of character development. Clearly, listeners need good vocabularies and a grounding in mathematics to appreciate much of the humor. We recommend a flexible approach when reading this aloud to a group. Try out the first two chapters and let your listeners' reactions determine whether you read on to the end or leave it for those children who are interested to finish independently.

Suggested Listening Level: Grades 4–6

The Piemakers BY HELEN CRESSWELL. *Illustrated by Judith Gwyn Brown.* New York: Macmillan, 1967.

Gravella Roller knew her father Arthy was the best piemaker in Danby Dale. All the Rollers were fine piemakers, whether the pie was beef or pork or pigeon, but the trouble was that Cousin Crispin of the Gorby Rollers was *also* considered a fine piemaker. So when the king declared a contest to find a pie "the biggest and the best by common consent," the honor of Danby Dale was at stake. The entire village turned out to help Arthy and his wife Jem prepare the biggest pie ever—enough to feed two thousand people.

There are inevitable problems with such a venture. The size of the pie dish, for instance, means it must be floated down the river to Danby, but with Arthy at the helm, one knows the Danby Rollers will triumph. This fanciful tale of the English Downs is as light as Arthy's pie crust and reads in about two and a half hours. Third- through sixth-grade listeners are appreciative of both the action and the aroma of a pie big enough to feed two thousand friends.

Suggested Listening Level: Grades 3–6

Portrait of Ivan   BY PAULA FOX.   *Illustrated by Saul Lambert.* Englewood Cliffs, N.J.: Bradbury Press, 1969.

Ivan's widowed father has commissioned an artist to paint his son's portrait. Through the growing relationship between the young artist and his subject, Ivan comes to new ways of seeing the world. Matt takes Ivan with him on a working trip to Florida where, messing about in a rowboat with a new friend, Ivan is for once free of adult supervision. By sketching an imagined scene of Ivan's mother's childhood, Matt helps Ivan fill the empty space that his father's grieving silence has created around her memory.

The story chronicles the gradual release of a boy from the safe but pent-up world of wealthy urban childhood. Yet every child who has begun to view the world differently from his or her parents, every child who has exchanged the comfortable, home-centered world of childhood for wider horizons, will understand what has happened to Ivan.

In this subtle, quiet book the meaning gradually accumulates. Some listeners will want to reread the book to ponder the questions Fox raises about human relationships and memory, about photography, drawing, and writing as ways of keeping alive the past. As in all of her distinguished fiction, this prize-winning author respects the acuteness and sensitivity of her young readers.

The eight chapters of the novel can be read in less than two hours.

Suggested Listening Level: Grades 4–6

The Pushcart War   BY JEAN MERRILL.   *Illustrated by Ronni Solbert.*   Boston: Addison-Wesley Publishing Co., 1964. Paperback: Dell, 1981.

Tension has been building in Manhattan. Overcrowded streets are to blame. Pushcart peddlers are tired of being shoved about by bullying trucks, and truck drivers are fed up with pushcarts taking up precious parking spaces. Then the mammoth trucking corporations declare war on the peddlers in secret, hoping to make them scapegoats for the public's anger. When Morris the Florist is knocked into a barrel of pickles by a Mighty Mammoth truck and his pushcart demolished, however, the peddlers decide to fight back. Events escalate into a hilarious epic battle, thanks to the peddlers' secret weapon—shooting tacks into truck tires with pea-shooters.

This is a clever and subtle David and Goliath story, a tongue-in-cheek account of a mythical war that will leave your audience thinking as well as smiling. It would be hard to name another book that is both as funny and as ultimately serious as this one.

The challenge for the reader is that the book is written as a history of a real event. There is extensive dialogue, and interspersed with the narrative are news bulletins, diary entries, and transcriptions of interviews. To be most effective, some preparation and practice is recommended. The thirty-six short chapters could be combined in groups of two or three.

Suggested Listening Level: Grades 3–7

Queenie Peavy BY ROBERT BURCH. *Illustrated by Jerry Lazare.* New York: The Viking Press, 1966. Paperback: Dell, 1980.

"Queenie Peavy was the only girl in Cotton Junction who could chew tobacco. She could also spit it—and with deadly aim. She could do a number of things with a considerable degree of accuracy, most of them unworthy of her attention." Hiding behind a tough veneer of pride, Queenie lives in the shadow of the federal penitentiary in Atlanta where her father is imprisoned. Through the sometimes painful events of the story, Queenie's idealized image of her father is gradually replaced by a recognition of him as he is. Queenie discovers that she can face life as *it* is, not just as she wants it to be. Yet she also learns that she can give pleasure to others with her singing and that her gentle touch with babies is appreciated. Queenie's prickly personality makes this an absorbing growing-up story that stays with one after the last chapter is read.

The microcosm of the junior high school world with

students, teachers, and principals, with assemblies and
wienie roasts, with gossip and cliques, is convincingly
portrayed. The chapters are episodic enough to provide natural divisions, but they can be combined for
seven or eight thirty-minute sessions. We recommend
this for fourth grade through eighth *and* family
groups.

Suggested Listening Level: Grades 4–8

A Racecourse for Andy BY PATRICIA WRIGHTSON.
Illustrated by Margaret Horder. New York: Harcourt
Brace Jovanovich, 1968.

Five boys have grown up playing together, so the
four others are patient and protective toward Andy,
as they gradually realize that he is retarded. It was as
if "Andy lived behind a closed window. When he
smiled his warm smile and spoke a little too loudly, it
was is if he were speaking through the glass." A
favorite game of the group is pretending to own and
swap various public buildings and facilities around
the city of Sydney; it is a game Andy can't seem to
understand and from which he feels left out.

Then one day an old tramp "sells" Andy the
Beecham Park Racecourse for three dollars, and Andy,
in all seriousness, believes himself the new owner.
Since those in authority at the racetrack let Andy come
and go as he pleases and indulge him in his fantasy, he
is proud and happy. The other boys, however, who
are afraid Andy's delusions will end up hurting him,
wrestle with difficult issues. Should they tell Andy the
truth and force him to face it? Are they just jealous of
his new privileges? Can anyone "own" greyhounds and

races and flowers anyway? The working-out of this
delicate predicament is handled with great sensitivity
by Patricia Wrightson, one of Australia's most distinguished writers for children.

The few Australian terms should pose no difficulty
for American children, as the context makes their
meaning clear. The book consists of twelve chapters,
each roughly ten to twelve minutes long.

Suggested Listening Level: Grades 4–7

Ramona the Pest BY BEVERLY CLEARY. *Illustrated
by Louis Darling.* New York: William Morrow &
Company, 1968. Paperback: Dell, 1982.

Ramona Quimby doesn't understand grown-ups.
How can mothers sigh that children grow up so
quickly when she's been waiting years just to get to
kindergarten? The first day of school doesn't quite
measure up to Ramona's high hopes, however. When
her teacher asks her to "sit here for the present,"
Ramona is disappointed because no "present" ma-
terializes. Then she has to sit out of the game just
because she pulled Susan's corkscrew curl to see if it
would go "boing." And she finds it especially difficult
to figure out what a dawnzer is in "Oh say can you see
by the dawnzer lee light."

Beverly Cleary's appreciation both of the intense
feelings small children experience and of the humor
in them has made her a perennial favorite with children. Though young readers usually prefer stories
about children their own age or slightly older, the
great popularity of *Ramona the Pest* and its sequels
shows that, like adults, children can enjoy looking

back through fiction at their younger selves and feeling fondly superior.

When read one chapter at a sitting, *Ramona the Pest* is a sure success with first- through third-graders (there are eight chapters in all). Of the sequels, *Ramona and Her Father* is particularly interesting, portraying family stress from a seven-year-old's perspective, when Mr. Quimby loses his job. *The Mouse and the Motorcycle* is another favorite Cleary book, especially with no-nonsense third-graders.

Suggested Listening Level: Grades K–3

Rascal: A Memoir of a Better Era BY STERLING NORTH. *Illustrated by John Schoenherr.* New York: E. P. Dutton & Co., 1963. Paperback: Avon Books, 1969.

Rascal, a young raccoon, is without a doubt one of the most winning pets ever to appear in a book. He eats in a high chair (when he's not walking across the table to dip into the sugar bowl) and rides in his young master's bicycle basket like an animated figurehead. Rascal's human-childlike qualities and the scrapes they get him into give him the appeal of a real-life Paddington Bear.

Rascal is more than a winsome pet story, however. North deftly captures the atmosphere of small-town Wisconsin during World War I and, even more vividly, the lavish beauty of northern farms, lakes, and streams. (North, boy and man, is a passionate fisherman.) In addition, the motherless child Sterling is a winning protagonist. Left alone a great deal by his lawyer father, Sterling is a poignant figure, but an enviable one as well. If he sometimes gets lonely, he also is allowed to take over the living room for months to build a large canoe. And his freedom to ramble about at will, with Rascal as an eager and curious companion, is an eleven-year-old's dream come true.

Each of the book's nine chapters makes a satisfying read-aloud session.

Suggested Listening Level: Grades 4–7

Red Fox   BY CHARLES G. D. ROBERTS.   *Illustrated by John Schoenherr.* Introduction by David McCord. Boston: Houghton Mifflin Company, 1905, 1972. Paperback: Dell, 1973.

Red Fox is a classic animal story given a new lease on life by its reissue a few years ago in an attractively illustrated version. Today's children who love animals and the wilderness should find the book as stirring as their grandparents did years ago.

In this account of the life of a fox, Roberts has confined himself to known and observed behaviors of foxes and has refrained from projecting human emotions onto animals. This strict authenticity in no way reduces either one's feeling for the protagonist or the suspense of the plot.

From the first chapter ("The Price of His Life"), in which Red Fox's father is killed leading two dogs away from his mate and five cubs, through "The Lessons of the Wild" that the young fox must learn, and his own mating, capture, and eventual clever escape, there is no scarcity of action. The story does proceed at a leisurely pace, however, over nineteen chapters, as Roberts spends many more words than a contemporary writer would dare to use describing the rugged

New Brunswick countryside or explaining some facet of animal behavior. This aspect of the book plus a challenging vocabulary and majestic periods in the prose reserve it for the experienced reader and listener. Those fortunate enough to share the story, however, will carry away indelible memories of the beauty and dignity of Red Fox and his world.

Suggested Listening Level: Grades 4-8

The Rescuers BY MARGERY SHARP. *Illustrated by Garth Williams.* Boston: Little, Brown and Company, 1959. Paperback: Dell, 1981.

Did you know that mice the world over have organized a Prisoners' Aid Society? Besides providing companionship and doing tricks to cheer those in prison, mice devote themselves to securing the liberty of unfortunate captives whenever possible. When Madam Chairwoman proposes that the Society take on the mission of freeing a Norwegian poet from the dungeons of the infamous Black Castle, however, the membership is dismayed. No mouse has been able to even reach the prisoners' cells there, the jailer's cat is "twice natural size and four times as fast," and none of them speaks Norwegian. But Madam Chairwoman has a plan, one that depends on an unlikely rescue party of Bernard, a rough but gallant pantry mouse, Nils, a seagoing Norwegian mouse recruited for the task, and Miss Bianca, the pampered pet of the Ambassador's son.

There is never a dull moment in the chronicle of their heroic adventure, and Margery Sharp's delightful prose style is a rare treat for both reader and listeners.

The fourteen chapters divide the book into manageable segments for reading sessions.

Suggested Listening Level: Grades 3–5

The Return of the Twelves BY PAULINE CLARKE. *Illustrated by Bernarda Bryson.*   First American edition, New York: Coward, McCann & Geoghegan, 1962 (out of print). Reprint, Boston: Gregg Press, 1980.

Max is the first to learn the secret of the twelve antique wooden soldiers tucked away in the attic of the English farmhouse to which the Morleys have just moved. Then his sister Jane and finally his older brother Phillip watch and listen to the twelve as they come alive and relate all manner of wondrous adventures. Butter Crashey, the Patriarch, "one hundred and forty years old and full of years and wisdom," tells the three Morley children enough about the soldiers' past to make it clear that the twelve once belonged to the Brontë children. The three Morleys read Branwell Brontë's *History of the Young Men* and decide to help the twelve return to their ancestral home, Haworth Parsonage, now a Brontë museum. When an American scholar threatens to take the soldiers to be displayed in the United States, the soldiers resolve to set out intrepidly across the English countryside to return to their rightful place on the Haworth mantel shelf.

This is a delightful reading experience for families. Like Mary Norton's *The Borrowers,* the speculation about life just beyond the corner of the eye is intriguing. The action here is very straightforward and can be handled in eight to ten sessions.

Suggested Listening Level: Grades 4–6

Roll of Thunder, Hear My Cry BY MILDRED D. TAYLOR. *Illustrated by Jerry Pinkney.* New York: The Dial Press, 1976. Paperback: Bantam Books, 1978.

This Newbery Medal-winning book tells of the good and bad times in the lives of the Logans, a family trying to hold on to their land in Mississippi during the Great Depression. Written by a young black woman, it is based on stories told by her father about his own boyhood. Through the dramatic events of the book, the young listener learns with nine-year-old Cassie Logan about the existence of bigotry and injustice. Yet the terror of night-riders and lynchings, the humiliation of insults and inferior schooling, are made bearable by the courage and warmth of the adult Logans. The suspense builds steadily to a haunting ending.

Mildred Taylor's relative inexperience as a writer at the time the book was written shows occasionally in an awkward phrase or clumsiness in narration (there is an excess of eavesdropping to maintain Cassie as the point-of-view character, for instance), but the suspense and emotional force of the story carry reader and listener over any rough spots. Fast-moving and touching, this novel has become a great favorite with children. A fairly good adaptation of the book was made for television. The novel is divided into twelve chapters, each suitable for one reading session.

Suggested Listening Level: Grades 4–6

Roller Skates BY RUTH SAWYER. *Illustrated by Valenti Angelo.* New York: The Viking Press, 1936. Paperback: Dell Books, 1969.

A whole year of freedom! Having seen her wealthy parents off to Europe and escaped the clutches of tyrannical Aunt Emily, Lucinda arrives to spend her "orphan year" with Miss Peters and Miss Nettie, as she says, "blissfully unhampered." Her roller skates take her all over New York City with all the exuberance of ten-year-old innocence as she makes delightful new friends: Mr. Gilligan and his hansom cab, Tony Coppino and the bambinos, and Trinket, a tiny child to cherish and share secrets with.

The story is based on the author's reminiscences of her own tenth year and catches for the reader/listener the poignancy of growing up. Although the setting of turn-of-the-century New York adds much to Lucinda's experiences (her excursions to Mr. Louis Sherry's for candy, for instance), it is Lucinda's face-to-face encounter with the death of Mrs. Grose and the even more searing loss of Trinket that raise her experiences above the commonplace.

The book begins with a rather coy introduction that we find more effective to omit or summarize, beginning the actual reading with chapter one. Episodic chapters provide easy divisions for eight or nine sessions.

Suggested Listening Level: Grades 4–6

Roosevelt Grady BY LOUISA SHOTWELL. *Illustrated by Peter Burchard.* New York: The World Publishing Company, 1963.

Roosevelt Grady knew a lot about schools. He'd been in nine different ones as his family followed the crops, from beans to cucumbers to fruits. Roosevelt liked school, but arithmetic in general and "putting into" in particular was a problem. The family never stayed any place long enough for him to find out about the finer points of "putting into." Roosevelt is long on planning, however, and shares a secret dream with his friend Manowar—that the family find a place to stay long enough for Mrs. Grady to put up curtains.

There are some references to events and circumstances of the early 1960s, "a rocking chair like President Kennedy's," for instance, and a rather rosy glow to the Gradys' life as "poor but honest pickers." On the other hand, Roosevelt and his warm, loving family transcend a particular era, and their hard work and belief in the value of education may provide a useful reminder to young listeners.

Suggested Listening Level: Grades 3–6

Rootabaga Stories BY CARL SANDBURG. 1922. Many editions.

In the Rootabaga Country the pigs wear bibs, and the railroad tracks change from straight to zigzag, and the mothers and fathers fix them. The biggest city in the big, big Rootabaga Country is the Village of Liver-and-Onions, and the Village of Cream Puffs is "a light little village on the upland corn prairie many miles past the sunset in the west." Here in the Rootabaga country, mothers and fathers and uncles and aunts tell stories about the Huckabuck Family, the Potato Face Blind Man, Jason Squiff the cistern cleaner, and the White Horse Girl and the Blue Wind Boy.

Sandburg's feel for the land and for the people of

the Midwest is evident in these nonsense stories. Most of the tales are rather short, taking no more than five or ten minutes to read, but the poet's ear for rhythm and alliteration make practice essential. While these stories may not appeal to every reader, listeners who are introduced to them will never hear a train whistle on a lonely Kansas prairie without remembering the two skyscrapers who had a child—and lost it.

Suggested Listening Level: Grades 4–8

The Saturdays BY ELIZABETH ENRIGHT. *Illustrated by the author.*   New York: Holt, Rinehart and Winston, 1941.   Paperback, Dell, 1977.

They were bored. The Melendy children had nothing to do, so they pooled their resources and formed I.S.A.A.C.—the Independent Saturday Afternoon Adventure Club. Each Saturday one of the four children (except for Oliver the youngest, of course) would go off to do whatever that person chose—ALONE. For each child, this independent venture turned out to be a step in self-discovery on the road to growing up. Many of the episodes are lively and suspenseful, as when Oliver decides he *isn't* too young to have his turn and goes off on his own to the circus. His adventure turns out well, as they all do, with a ride home on a policeman's horse.

Those middle-class children who live under close parental supervision will envy the Melendy children the autonomy granted to them by their father and the housekeeper, both of whom Mrs. Enright wisely keeps offstage through most of the book.

There is a bit of nostalgia here because the 1939 setting obviously involves the New York City that the author knew well. At the same time, there is a freshness and spontaneity to these gentle adventures that may lure the shy listener to vicarious participation. Each of the eight chapters requires about forty minutes' reading time.

Suggested Listening Level: Grades 4–6

The Secret Garden BY FRANCES HODGSON BURNETT. *Illustrated by Tasha Tudor.* 1909. New York: J. B. Lippincott Company, 1962. Paperback: Dell, 1971.

Mary Lennox is a very unattractive child—thin, pale, and sour-looking. To make things worse, when we meet her at the opening of the story, she is "as tyrannical and selfish a little pig as ever lived." The transformation of this unlikely heroine into a lively, loving, and attractive child is the subject of *The Secret Garden*. When a cholera epidemic leaves Mary suddenly orphaned, she is sent from India to a huge old manor house in Yorkshire, the home of her uncle. A mysterious, brooding figure, he is rarely at home and shows no interest in the child.

In this pathetic state, Mary might be expected to become more disagreeable than ever. That she does not is due to her discovery of Colin, an invalid cousin shut away in the recesses of the mansion, of robust and cheerful Dickon with his gift of nurturing plant and animal life, and of the growing things that transform the bleak Yorkshire winter into luxuriant spring. Together the three children bring back to life the walled garden that Mr. Craven has shut up since his wife's death ten years earlier, and the garden in turn brings Colin to health and Mr. Craven out of his grief.

The story is both a hymn of tribute to the healing power of the natural world and a psychologically acute study. Its "happily ever after" resolution is as satisfying as the best fairy tale.

The Yorkshire dialect that is spoken by some of the characters looks a bit intimidating on the page, but it's easier to manage than it looks once you get under way. The book has twenty-seven chapters averaging fifteen minutes apiece. Although this makes it longer than the typical children's book today, most children become caught up in the story and enjoy every minute of it.

Suggested Listening Level: Grades 4–7

Shadow of a Bull   BY MAIA WOJCIECHOWSKA.   *Illustrated by Alvin Smith.*   New York: Atheneum, 1964. Paperback: Atheneum, 1972.

In the small Spanish town of Arcangel, the people all long for the day when Manolo, the son of a great bullfighter, is himself old enough to fight bulls. They are sure he will be as great as his father, who ten years ago was killed in the bullring—and then the town will be famous and full of life again. But Manolo has no desire to fight bulls, nothing like the fierce desire that makes his friend Juan willing to take any risks to face the magnificent, terrible animals. Manolo is full of fear. He sees no way to escape his fate, however, for six men who have been good to Manolo and his mother, followers of his father's career, have taught him all they know about bullfighting; he cannot disappoint them.

Tension builds relentlessly in the book as the time for Manolo to face his first bull approaches, and the climactic scene is orchestrated skillfully. The world of bullfighting and its meaning to Spaniards is so vividly realized that the novel far transcends the subject of physical courage; it is a novel about discovering one's identity and claiming it.

The book consists of fifteen short chapters and a helpful glossary defining bullfighting terms and indicating their pronunciation.

Suggested Listening Level: Grades 4–6

The Shrinking of Treehorn BY FLORENCE PARRY HEIDE. *Illustrated by Edward Gorey.* New York: Holiday House, 1971. Paperback: Dell, 1980.

Nobody's listening. Children all suspect this, but Treehorn knows it better than most as he shrinks in size day by day, until he is small enough to stand under the bed and play a game "to grow on." Nobody listens to him. His mother and father urge him to behave. His teacher suggests that shrinking is inappropriate behavior in her classroom. Bus drivers, even good friends, pay no attention to the *real* Treehorn.

This short, sophisticated story will strike a chord in anyone who has ever been ignored. It is deceptive in its simplicity and should be shared with older groups, fourth or fifth grades through junior high. For families, it may be a source of much discussion. Edward

Gorey's illustrations add to the wry humor of Tree-horn's problem, but the story line moves successfully on its own.

Suggested Listening Level: Grades 4–7

Slake's Limbo BY FELICE HOLMAN. New York: Charles Scribner's Sons, 1974. Paperback: Dell, 1981.

> . . . It is simplest and most practical to believe that Slake was born an orphan at the age of thirteen, small, near-sighted, dreaming, bruised, an outlander in the city of his birth (and in the world), a lad of sifting fitful faith with a token in his pocket. In other ways he was not so different from the rest of the young raised with house keys around their necks, rearing themselves in litter-strewn streets.

So Aremis Slake, repeatedly harassed by a gang in his neighborhood, takes refuge in New York's subway and there survives for one hundred twenty-one days. Willis Joe Whinney, a motorman on the subway, also seeks refuge from his world in dreams about sheep ranching in Australia. Willis Joe and Slake have only one chance encounter, but each is changed, and as the book draws to a close, the reader/listener catches sight of the bright blue sky that pulls Slake back into the world above the subway.

Slake's story is a dramatic, moving one that can catch the reader on many levels. Daily routines estab-lished by Slake simply to exist are intriguing, but more than that, the isolation of an individual in a crowded, rushed society is starkly revealed. This is not a happy book, but it is compelling. The relatively short narrative can be broken after chapters three, seven, eleven, and thirteen into approximately twenty- to thirty-minute sessions.

Suggested Listening Level: Grades 6-8

Sounder BY WILLIAM ARMSTRONG. *Illustrated by James Barkley.* New York: Harper & Row, 1969. Paperback: Harper & Row, 1972.

Sounder contains some of the most painful scenes in children's fiction, yet, as in classic tragedy, the beauty of the language and the stature of the characters transform the story into an uplifting experience. A boy stands helplessly by as sheriff's men brutally arrest his father and shoot the family's magnificent coonhound, Sounder. The father, a sharecropper, has in desperation stolen a ham to feed his hungry family. Though grievously wounded in the head, the dog survives, restless and mute, waiting six long years for the return of his master from a chain gang. All that while, the boy searches for his father, whenever the field work allows. The family is finally reunited, but both the father and the dog soon die of their injuries. A note of hope lingers, however: the education that the boy has been able to acquire promises a way out of the inhuman oppression the family has known.

Just as medieval morality plays portrayed the life of Everyman to dramatize universal events and emotions, so the loyalty and long suffering of the dog Sounder serve to dramatize the dignity and long suffering of this poor black family. Some critics have felt that Armstrong's decision not to give the characters names demeans them, but children recognize the love and trust and endurance of this family that just might be Everyfamily. Little more than two hours' reading time is required, but don't rush this one. Allow time for discussion, for thought, for tears.

Suggested Listening Level: Grades 5–8

Soup BY ROBERT NEWTON PECK. *Illustrated by Charles C. Gehm.*   New York: Alfred A. Knopf, 1974. Paperback: Dell, 1981.

Boyhood pleasures in the rural Vermont of the 1920s are celebrated in this engaging small volume: a good piece of rope, small green apples and sassafras whips to send them flying, acorn pipes and cornsilk tobacco. The boys in question are the narrator and his best friend, Soup, who is "a regular genius" at getting the boys in trouble. One hilarious episode in the "bad boy" vein follows another until the last chapter adds a new and touching dimension to the boys' friendship.

Peck's language is as high-spirited as the boys' antics —richly figurative in a robust, down-to-earth idiom. The author, who drew on memories of his own childhood for *Soup* and its sequel, zeroes in perfectly on third-grade psychology, even to the bathroom humor with which the boys frequently regale each other. Young listeners will love it, but adults who prefer to avoid the vulgar terms for bodily functions may find themselves uncomfortable with this book. Grandparents not averse to letting their hair down, however, will particularly enjoy sharing with children Peck's nostalgic vignettes of days gone by.

The ten very brief chapters can be read aloud in about one hour.

Suggested Listening Level: Grades 3–5

A Stranger at Green Knowe BY LUCY BOSTON. *Illustrated by Peter Boston.* New York: Harcourt Brace & World, 1961. Paperback: Harcourt Brace Jovanovich, 1979.

Ping, a Chinese orphan refugee, visits the monkey house of the London zoo. The miserable creatures depress him until he catches sight of the magnificent gorilla, Hanno, like him taken from the beautiful forest to live in a world of concrete. Hanno's power and noble rage move Ping deeply and he, quite simply, falls in love. Later, Ping is invited by elderly Mrs. Oldknowe to visit her centuries-old home, complete with moat. While Ping is there, Hanno escapes and makes his way north, taking refuge in the bamboo thickets within the moat at Green Knowe. There Ping tries to protect him from capture. Though this is not possible—there is no place for Hanno in our world—Ping does provide the great beast with companionship and freedom for a few precious days.

Many elements combine to make this a superb novel. The description in the opening pages of a gorilla family's life in the equatorial jungle and its destruction in the terror of pursuit and capture will remain with the reader always. The relationship between the old lady and the gentle child is developed with remarkable subtlety. In addition, Mrs. Boston's courage in raising profound questions without supplying easy answers contributes to the deeply moving story.

Lucy Boston, who lives in the nine-hundred-year-old house that she writes about, has set other novels at Green Knowe in which Ping, Mrs. Oldknowe, and other characters figure. Each volume is quite different; all reflect the skill and intelligence of a remarkable writer.

A Stranger at Green Knowe is divided into three unequal parts. Parts One and Two can each be read in one long session (about forty minutes apiece) or two shorter sessions. The long final part contains frequent breaks that provide logical stopping places. Total time to read the book aloud is estimated at just under three hours.

Suggested Listening Level: Grades 4–8

A Stranger Came Ashore BY MOLLIE HUNTER.   New York: Harper & Row, 1975. Paperback: Harper & Row, 1977.

In the Shetland Islands there are many stories about the selkies, the seals who take human shape and live on the land for a time. It is said that the selkies aren't really animals but a kind of folk doomed to live in the sea. Fallen angels they are, and they're ruled by a great bull seal who lives in a jeweled palace and lures golden-haired young lasses to his kingdom. Anyway, this is the tale told to Robbie Henderson by his Old Da when Robbie shares with his grandfather his uneasiness about the shipwrecked sailor, Finn Learson. And Robbie's sister Elspeth has golden hair and seems bedazzled by the dark-eyed stranger. The tangled threads don't sort themselves out, however, until the final night of the Christmas festival when Robbie and Elspeth and Finn Learson each fight for what they want.

This is definitely a "page-turner." The action and suspense build page by page, and fourth- through sixth-graders will hardly allow stopping for a sip of water. The setting is as authentic as master Scottish storyteller Mollie Hunter can make it; even landlocked listeners will be able to hear sea breakers pounding on the rocky shore.

Suggested Listening Level: Grades 4–7

Striped Ice Cream   BY JOAN LEXAU.   *Illustrated by John Wilson.*   Philadelphia and New York: J. B. Lippincott Company, 1968.

In *Striped Ice Cream,* Joan Lexau has captured the hurts that come with being the youngest in a family of several children. Seven-year-old Becky "spent a lot of time thinking that no matter how old she got, she would never catch up to the others"—her four older siblings. Soon it will be Becky's birthday, and because all of the children need new shoes, Becky fears there will be no presents and none of her favorite "striped ice cream" on her birthday. Her sisters and brother manage to make her a special birthday gift, but their efforts to keep it a secret make Becky feel more left out than ever. Yet it all comes around to a happy ending.

Mrs. Lexau handles sensitively the subject of a "father-absent" black family struggling to obtain the necessities of life while keeping its pride intact. The

loving warmth of the close-knit family remind one of
The Moffats and *All-of-a-Kind-Family*. Reading time
is approximately two hours.

Suggested Listening Level: Grades 2–5

The Sword and the Grail   RETOLD BY CONSTANCE
HIEATT.   *Illustrated by David Palladini.*   New York:
Thomas Y. Crowell Publishers, 1972.

This Arthurian story of the quest for the grail is
Constance Hieatt's reworking of many ancient and
often conflicting tales on the subject. Since she is a
sensitive writer for children as well as a medieval
scholar, the result is a compelling story.

In the days of King Arthur, a boy named Perceval
grows up never having heard of the Round Table or
even of knighthood itself. His widowed mother has
kept him in the remote mountains of Wales, far from
the dangerous court life that was her husband's un-
doing; but when, by chance, the fair young Perceval
sees a party of knights, he is dazzled by their glory.
Forsaking his poor mother, he sets out for Arthur's
court to become a knight. He has much to learn and
many trials to meet, however, before he is worthy of
his destiny as healer of the Fisher King and leader of
the Company of the Grail.

Perceval's ignorance of courtly ways often leads him
into humorous predicaments, which leaven the basic
solemnity of the story. Hieatt's successful retelling of
this and several other medieval tales can go a long
way toward satisfying children's thirst for and interest
in heroes. *The Sword and the Grail* is divided into ten

short chapters. Palladini's illustrations are thoroughly
elegant.

Suggested Listening Level: Grades 4–8

Tatterhood and Other Tales EDITED BY ETHEL JOHN-
STON PHELPS. *Illustrated by Pamela Baldwin Ford.*
Old Westbury, N.Y.: The Feminist Press, 1978. Paper-
back: The Feminist Press, 1978.

Because the influential collections of fairy tales for
children were edited by Victorian gentlemen like
Andrew Lang and Joseph Jacobs, the tales best known
to us feature beautiful passive young women waiting
for handsome brave young men to rescue them from
difficulties. The only strong women in these tales tend
to be old, ugly, and evil. Such stories reinforced the
Victorian ideal of masculinity and femininity as polar
opposites. In recent years, students of folklore have
discovered many tales that depict women and men in
more varied roles, and the best of these tales are as
appealing as the old favorites. Several collections of
folktales have appeared by now that feature appealing,
active women—young and old, pretty and plain. *Tatterhood and Other Tales* is one of the best. Included
in it are the comical Japanese tall tale of "Three Strong
Women" who train a great wrestler; "Unanana and the
Elephant," an African tale of a clever woman who
rescues her children from an elephant's belly; and
"Kate Crackernuts," a Scottish tale that depicts the
devotion between two step-sisters as one endures
great dangers to free the other from an evil spell. The
collection is wider ranging than most: tales from

Egypt, Ecuador, China, and a California native American tribe are included as well as European tales.

Nothing can or should take the place of such tales as "Cinderella" and "Snow White," stories of deep power and beauty. These twenty-five tales provide, however, an ideal supplement to the traditional fairy tale collections.

Suggested Listening Level: Grades K–8

Thank You, Jackie Robinson BY BARBARA COHEN. *Illustrated by Richard Cuffari.*   New York: Lothrop, Lee & Shepard, 1974.

Sam Greene leads a solitary life in a family of two big sisters and a busy widowed mother who runs an inn. Then a new cook arrives, an elderly black man who shares Sam's passion for the Brooklyn Dodgers. The two become friends as they listen to broadcasts of the Dodger games and root for their favorite player, rookie Jackie Robinson. Davy and his daughter take Sam to his first Dodger game, and then Sam and Davy travel to other ballparks where the Dodgers are playing. When Davy has a heart attack, Sam overcomes his shyness to approach Jackie Robinson before a game and have a ball autographed for his friend. Sam gradually comes to realize what Jackie Robinson's success means to a sixty-year-old black man. And it is Jackie Robinson's grace and his courage against the odds of injustice and of time itself that alone comfort Sam after Davy's death.

The play-by-play action that figures occasionally in the book may intimidate readers and listeners who are not baseball fans, but don't be put off, for *Thank You,*

Jackie Robinson, like all the best sports fiction, is much more than a sports story. It can be read in five or six twenty-minute sessions.

Suggested Listening Level: Grades 3–6

Thistle and Thyme: Tales and Legends from Scotland BY SORCHE NIC LEODHAS (pseud. Leclaire Alger). *Illustrated by Evaline Ness.* New York: Holt, Rinehart and Winston, 1962 (out of print).

Whether it's humor you want or romance, tales of the fairy folk or of ancient monks and pirates, you'll find in this collection a story to suit you. Sorche Nic Leodhas has skillfully preserved the lilt and resonance of the original Gaelic; the tales are a joy to read aloud. Whichever story you choose, within minutes your audience will be hanging on every word. Notice, for instance, the sprightly pace with which "The Laird's Lass and the Gobha's Son" starts out:

> An old laird had a young daughter once and she was the pawkiest piece in all the world. Her father petted her and her mother cosseted her till the wonder of it was that she wasn't so spoiled that she couldn't be borne. What saved her from it was that she was so sunny and sweet by nature, and she had a naughty merry way about her that won all hearts. The only thing wrong with her was that when she set her heart on something she'd not give up till she got what it was she wanted.

What she sets her heart on, of course, is marrying the gobha's (or blacksmith's) son, and thereby hangs the tale.

This book of ten stories is our favorite of several folktale collections by the same author, but the other volumes have many appealing stories also.

Suggested Listening Level: Grades 2–8

A Toad for Tuesday BY RUSSELL ERICKSON. *Illustrated by Lawrence Di Fiori.* New York: Lothrop, Lee & Shephard, 1974. Paperback: Dell, 1975.

Everyone knows toads don't go out in winter—not even to deliver the finest of beetle brittle to dear old Aunt Toolia. But Warton did go out on a sunny winter's day and began an adventure that nearly cost him his life, though it won him an unlikely new friend.

In the world of anthropomorphized creatures, two toads, Warton and Morton, an owl named George, and an army of mice on skis led by an intrepid adventurer named Sy are not only believable but deftly define human foibles and follies. This sprightly tale can be read in two sessions: a break naturally occurs after the first cup of clover blossom tea shared by George and Warton. It is suitable for the primary grades, although for kindergarten listeners you may wish to read it in three sessions.

Suggested Listening Level: Grades K–3

Tom's Midnight Garden BY PHILIPPA PEARCE. Philadelphia and New York: J. B. Lippincott Company, 1959 (out of print). Paperback: Dell, 1979.

What does it mean when a clock strikes thirteen? Tom, who has been exiled during his brother's illness to the dreary little flat of Aunt Gwen and Uncle Tom, finds the thirteenth hour allows him to walk into a garden that doesn't exist—at least not in this time. The garden is part of the lawn that surrounded the building sixty years before when it was a mansion. Whenever the clock invites him, Tom enters the midnight garden and plays with the mysterious little girl he meets there. As his expeditions continue he discovers that although *he* doesn't change, the young girl, Hatty, does. She is growing older. As the time for Tom to return to his family approaches, Hatty is a young woman about to be married and the bond between the two seems to be weakening. Tom wants desperately to see her once more, to prove that the garden is more than a dream. When his need evokes a glimpse of the real Hatty, Tom at last understands the mystery of the garden.

Pearce not only develops this as an adventure story, but offers an intriguing speculation on the nature of time. She transforms the inescapable fact of growing old from an abstraction beyond children's grasp to a moving reality. British critic John Rowe Townsend has termed *Tom's Midnight Garden* the best English children's book since World War II. It is not a first book to read aloud, for listeners will need some patience with the beginning, but it goes very well in eight or nine sessions for middle grades. It is also deeply satisfying family fare.

Suggested Listening Level: Grades 5–8

Treasure Island   BY ROBERT LOUIS STEVENSON.   1883. Many editions.

This classic tale hasn't lost a bit of its appeal in one hundred years. The tarry pigtails and bloody dirks of the motley pirate crew, the unique mixture of irresistible charm and malevolence that is Long John Silver, and the enviable, plucky Jim Hawkins are as vivid today as when Stevenson created them for the amusement of his adolescent stepson during a rainy stay in Scotland. Jim's adventure is a child's fantasy come true. At the story's start, Jim leads a humdrum life as an innkeeper's son, but the arrival and subsequent death of an irascible old pirate brings ample excitement and danger, for Jim comes into possession of a treasure map left by the old buccaneer. On the voyage to find the treasure, mutiny and murder repeatedly threaten, but Jim, through luck, wit, and daring, saves the day time and again.

Some girls think they won't like *Treasure Island*, perhaps because it's so often labeled "a boy's book." Yet if they can be persuaded to keep an open mind, they'll soon be scrambling into the mizzen shrouds with Jim, and puzzling over the enigma of Long John Silver.

Don't worry about understanding all the nautical language. It supplies flavor and authenticity, but knowing every term isn't necessary for an understanding of the plot. The book consists of thirty-four chapters arranged in six parts. If your listeners' attention spans hold out, three chapters at a session works well.

Suggested Listening Level: Grades 5–8

Tuck Everlasting BY NATALIE BABBITT. New York: Farrar, Straus & Giroux, 1975. Paperback: Bantam Books, 1976.

Hot, dusty days of August, days that "hang at the top of summer," enclose the events that bring the Tuck family and ten-year-old Winnie Foster together. When Winnie decides to run away from her nagging family, she stumbles across Jesse Tuck and his secret bubbling pool of water that has given the Tuck family immortality. They never grow older, never become sick, and, of course, never die. In short, they never change. But life *is* change, and as Tuck himself says, "You can't call it living what we got. We just *are,* we just be." Their ominous secret is sought after by an outsider who wants to exploit the water. In a violent confrontation with the Tucks, the man is killed. Winnie realizes the necessity of keeping the secret and protecting the Tucks, but she must also decide whether or not to join them by drinking the water herself.

The wooded setting and the hot humid weather pervade this speculative, thought-provoking fantasy. The action is fast enough for even beginning listeners, and the story can be read in three or four twenty-minute sessions. Yet Winnie's forced choice between immortality and growing old is intriguing enough to capture the interest of a family or a group with a wide age range. This paperback would be a perfect addition to a backpack on a camping trip.

Suggested Listening Level: Grades 3–8

Watership Down BY RICHARD ADAMS. New York: Macmillan, 1975. Paperback: Avon Books, 1975.

In a peaceful rabbit warren, a young rabbit has a premonition of terrible danger (which turns out to be the gassing of the rabbits and destruction of the warren to make way for a housing development). The chief rabbit ignores young Fiver's advice to evacuate, so Fiver and his brother Hazel lead a small group of rabbits on a journey to find a new home. Their odyssey is full of perils—their natural enemies, their own fears and habits, hostile rabbits. Comforted and heartened by the legends of their shrewd ancestor rabbit, however, they survive to found a new and more humane (if one may use that word) warren.

The rabbits Adams depicts are true to rabbit behavior and yet each is fully individualized, and the listener quickly becomes deeply involved in the fate of the stalwart band. Adams even invents a rabbit language, for which he provides a glossary, but one soon finds rabbit words incorporated into one's own vocabulary.

The book is easy to criticize. The title (which refers to the location of the new warren) does not attract the reader. Adams indulges too much in ruminating digressions (they can be skipped so as not to lose the attention of the audience). Moreover, his is an old English clubman's view of the world. Creatures the rabbits view as inferior "talk funny"—in this case, broken English with a Mediterranean accent and occasional vulgar phrases. And females seem to be an afterthought with Adams, as they are with his rabbits, who never think of including females in their community until they are ready to breed. Yet when all is said and done, *Watership Down* is an absorbing read and a remarkable achievement.

The epigraphs that begin each chapter, taken from such towering figures as Aeschylus, Shakespeare, and Jane Austen, may be over the heads of some children but are worth reading aloud (when possible; some are not translated into English). They add to the solemn atmosphere of the saga. This is a long book: fifty chapters and a brief epilogue.

Suggested Listening Level: Grades 5–8

Westmark BY LLOYD ALEXANDER. New York: E. P. Dutton & Co., 1981. Paperback: Dell, 1982.

Like many of Lloyd Alexander's best books, *Westmark* is about political power and personal morality. In this case, these issues are embodied in a dashing plot enacted by a motley crew of characters: a grief-stricken king manipulated by an evil prime minister; a lovable charlatan; a female street waif of mysterious origins and strange powers; young revolutionaries; and an appealing adolescent hero—Theo, a printer's devil or apprentice. One hair-raising episode follows another in the pell-mell plot until the author neatly gathers up all the threads in a surprising yet satisfying resolution.

The twenty-nine chapters of *Westmark* are very short (five to seven pages in most cases), so they can be combined to suit the time available for a reading session. The book's division into four parts should be observed by making a part-ending coincide with the end of a reading session whenever possible. Total reading-aloud time is approximately eight hours. Fantasy buffs may also want to try Alexander's famous

Prydain series—a five-book cycle based loosely on Welsh legend.

Suggested Listening Level: Grades 5–8

The Wheel on the School BY MEINDERT DEJONG. *Illustrated by Maurice Sendak.* New York: Harper & Brothers, 1954. Paperback: Harper & Brothers, 1972.

Everyone knows that storks bring good luck to the houses they nest on, but until Lina writes a composition about storks, none of the six children in the Dutch village school wonder why no storks nest in Shora. When they begin to wonder, things begin to happen. Before long the entire village is caught up in the search for a wagon wheel, which, placed on top of a peaked Shora roof, can serve as a platform for a stork's nest. The strength and wits of everyone are needed to find, repair, and mount the wheel, then to rescue two storm-tossed storks from drowning.

Although the story takes place far away—in a treeless village rimmed with dikes—and long ago—when women and even little girls wore heavy, billowing skirts that hindered their activity—Meindert DeJong penetrates straight to universal feelings of childhood that transcend all surface differences.

Of DeJong's many other books, *Shadrach* is particularly appealing in its sensitive depiction of a little child's intense longing for a pet. *The House of Sixty Fathers* is a grim but powerful account of a Chinese boy who is separated from his family at the time of the Japanese invasion.

The fifteen chapters of *The Wheel on the School* make it quite long for the audience to whom it will most appeal: seven- to nine-year-olds. Children who are good listeners, however, will be captivated by it.

Suggested Listening Level: Grades 2–4

Where the Lilies Bloom BY VERA AND BILL CLEAVER. Philadelphia and New York: J. B. Lippincott Company, 1969. Paperback: The New American Library, 1974.

Set in the Great Smoky Mountains of North Carolina, this is the story of Mary Call Luther, a feisty, nononsense fourteen-year-old. Hungry for education, she finds her ambitions are thwarted by her responsibilities. She worries about her older sister, "cloudy-headed" Devola, "so free and innocent, so womanly in form but with a child's heart and a child's mind," about Ima Dean and Romey, "so carefree . . . with never a thought in their little heads as to how they're going to get decently raised," and about her sharecropper father, "coughing his life away." The story is told in Mary Call's forthright, eloquent voice, and seldom has a first-person narration achieved such moving intimacy. "And I get scared and I think but how am I going to do this? Who will show me how and who will help me?" she asks.

The struggles of the children to keep their father's death a secret from the authorities and to survive the winter make compelling reading. Part of the solution is found in the ancient art of wildcrafting, gathering and selling medicinal roots and herbs from the mountains. Another part is Mary Call's learning to accept help from others. The Cleavers have written many other books, some of them very good ones, but none equal this story of the "wondrous glory" and "awful anxiety" of independence. Each of the fifteen chapters would make a good read-aloud session, but your listeners probably won't let you stop with just one.

Suggested Listening Level: Grades 4–8

The White Archer: An Eskimo Legend BY JAMES HOUSTON. *Illustrated by the author.* New York: Harcourt Brace & World, 1967. Paperback: Harcourt Brace Jovanovich, 1979.

The Eskimo boy Kungo escapes when Indian warriors massacre his parents and take his sister into captivity. The family's only offense had been extending the customary hospitality to travelers, not knowing them to be raiders of an Indian camp.

With the bloody scene stamped on his memory, the boy prepares himself for revenge. He travels to a distant island where an old man and woman take him in. The old man undertakes to make Kungo into a great archer. It is a slow process and Kungo is often impatient, but after four years he has become a great archer and a man. Kungo then sets out to exercise his vengeance. He learns, however, when he reaches the Indian camp that his sister has been adopted by the tribe and is married to a young warrior. The tale's benign resolution holds no surprises, but the endless cycle that violence spawns needs to be discovered anew by each person; it is a theme worth repeating.

Middle-school readers will be stirred by the book's issues of loyalty and justice. Houston includes much detail about Eskimo ways, however, so the book requires an audience of willing and thoughtful listeners.

James Houston is a Canadian artist who for years lived with Eskimos, helping in the development of Inuit art. He has done us a comparable service in retelling for the rest of the world this and other Eskimo legends.

The White Archer has no chapter divisions, so the reader should plan ahead for breaks in the reading sessions. The entire book can be read in about two hours.

Suggested Listening Level: Grades 5–8

The White Mountains   BY JOHN CHRISTOPHER.   New York: Macmillan, 1967.   Paperback: Macmillan, 1970.

Will Parker's friend Jack was the only one who asked questions or wondered about why things were the way they were. But he didn't ask any more questions after the Capping Ceremony, a ceremony that changed young people into followers of the system imposed by the Tripods. *No* one questioned the rules and regulations of life in the small villages and towns dotting the English countryside, not even the mindless vagrants who wandered about after their capping had somehow failed. One day, however, Will is approached by a vagrant who is not at all what he appears to be, a wanderer who persuades Will that there is hope for a better, freer life if he can just reach the White Mountains.

Set in an indefinite future time, this taut adventure story will capture readers just as surely as the machine-like Tripods dominate the humans they cap. Listeners will be intrigued with the artifacts from an earlier civilization, such as Watches and railroad tracks that are discovered by Will and his two companions as they journey to the stronghold in the mountains. The ten chapters, each about twenty to twenty-five minutes, are episodic enough to form good breaks, but we recommend that you plan some longer sessions in anticipation of audience demand. Will's story is continued in *The Pool of Fire* and *City of Gold and Lead*.

Suggested Listening Level: Grades 4–6

Wild Animals, Gentle Women   BY MARGERY FACKLAM. New York: Harcourt Brace Jovanovich, 1978.

What do giant pandas, owls, sharks, dolphins, chimpanzees, beavers, or white whales have in common? Each was studied by a woman and each is featured in a chapter in this book about the scientific contributions of these eleven naturalists. While each chapter depicts a distinct individual, together they subtly convey the qualities of an effective scientist. "The more they watch and the more they think they know about an animal, the more questions they find to ask."

The lively anecdotal style of writing makes this an ideal choice for reading aloud, for there is enough action in these accounts to interest even the most resistant nature lover. The first chapter is a general introduction to ethology, and if you choose to skip around in the book or to read chapters on widely scattered occasions, we recommend summarizing it. An interesting ploy would be to precede Farley Mowat's *Owls in the Family* with chapter five: "Kay McKeever and a Parliament of Owls." Each of the accounts requires approximately fifteen to twenty minutes' reading time.

Suggested Listening Level: Grades 3–8

The Wind in the Willows BY KENNETH GRAHAME, 1908. *Illustrated by Ernest H. Shepard.* New York: Charles Scribner's Sons, 1933. Paperback: Many editions.

From the moment Mole flings down his spring-cleaning tools, follows the imperious call of spring, and catches his first glimpse of the river, *The Wind in the Willows* casts a powerful spell. Few writers can match Grahame's skill at evoking the beauty of the natural world, the love of one's own home-place, and the charm of small wild creatures. The story consists of two plot-threads, each with its distinctive mood. There are the mellow and lyrical chapters devoted primarily to the friendship and activities of Mole and Ratty. The chapters that star the rich and swaggering yet good-natured Toad, on the other hand, are humorous, even lapsing into slapstick at times. The threads frequently overlap and then come together in the last part of the book, the epic battle of Toad Hall.

The story originated as episodes in a bedtime story that was continued by letter when Grahame's son Alistair was away on holiday; it is tailor-made for reading aloud. Yet action is minimal in some chapters, and not everyone has a taste for Grahame's highly wrought prose. We therefore don't recommend it for all groups of children (though they might enjoy one of the livelier chapters, such as "The Open Road"). It well deserves its reputation as a classic, however, and will please some children—and adults—like no other book in the world.

Suggested Listening Level: Grades 2–8

Winnie-the-Pooh BY A. A. MILNE. *Illustrated by Ernest H. Shepard.* New York: E. P. Dutton & Co., 1926. Paperback: Dell, 1982.

These whimsical tales of young Christopher Robin and his friends Pooh and Piglet, Eeyore, Rabbit, Owl, Kanga and Roo, have entered the lore of childhood all over the English-speaking world. Much in the stories is provided for the adult reader's amusement. As a result, a patronizing tone creeps in occasionally that may make some readers uncomfortable. Yet there is plenty here to delight the child listener: the appealing fantasy of toys come to life; Christopher Robin's superior adult-like role as brave and wise protector to all the others; the sharply drawn personalities of the toy animals.

Film versions and abridged editions of these stories abound. Be sure that your children's acquaintance with Pooh doesn't end with them. The great distinction of the stories is Milne's skillfully crafted language, both in the prose and in the verses that are scattered through the chapters, and for that, you must seek out the original.

The ten chapters provide ten reading sessions, each

concluding with a comforting resolution that makes the stories good bedtime fare.

Suggested Listening Level: Grades K–3

The Witch of Blackbird Pond BY ELIZABETH SPEARE. Boston: Houghton Mifflin Company, 1958. Paperback: Dell, 1972.

Imagine stepping from a life of cultured ease on a Caribbean plantation into the grim piety and primitive conditions of colonial Connecticut in 1687. This is the trying experience of Kit Tyler, who is forced to leave sunny Barbados when her grandfather dies in debt. Kit goes to her only other relatives, her aunt's family in a cold and unfriendly New England. The family takes her in but is shocked by her secular ways and frivolous clothes. Kit must cope with unaccustomed drudgery, a cousin's jealousy, and a disapproving community. A wealthy suitor offers her a quick way to respectability, but she resists that temptation. Her only comfort and understanding come from another outcast, an old Quaker woman, rumored to be a witch, who lives alone on the flats near Blackbird Pond. In the gripping climax of the story, Kit saves old Hannah from an ignorant mob, but she is then tried for witchcraft herself.

Because most American women in years gone by led uneventful domestic lives subordinated to men, the great majority of American historical novels for children have featured male protagonists. In *The Witch of Blackbird Pond,* Elizabeth Speare has created an active, adventurous heroine without violating the carefully developed seventeenth-century setting. The twenty-one chapters could be read one at a time or in groups of two.

Suggested Listening Level: Grades 5–8

The Wizard of Earthsea   BY URSULA LE GUIN.   *Illustrated by Ruth Robbins.*   New York: Houghton Mifflin, Parnassus Press, 1968.   Paperback: Bantam Books, 1982.

In the wide-flung island world of Earthsea, a boy discovers that he has the power to call a falcon from the sky or to work the weather to protect his village from pillaging raiders. These are Duny's first steps toward becoming a mage, one of the greatest of all mages. The path to greatness takes him through great pain and peril, however, even to "the lightless coasts of death's kingdom." At the School for Wizards, Ged (as Duny is now called) is taught that magic is not for entertainment or for power but "must follow knowledge and serve need." When challenged to a contest of powers by a despised rival, however, Ged rashly ignores this lesson and, in doing so, looses an awful evil on the world. From then on, this horror pursues him until he turns in desperation to face it. The courage he musters and the lesson he learns in that moment make him worthy at last of his great gifts.

In this gripping and profound fantasy, Le Guin has created an elaborate world, conjured up by lovely and suggestive place-names. In a classroom reading some students may be intimidated by all the names, in fact, so it is a good idea to reassure them that they can sit back and enjoy the story—there will be no tests on the geography of Earthsea. *The Wizard of Earthsea* is the first of a trilogy, but it is totally self-contained and stands on its own. We recommend ten reading sessions, one for each longish chapter.

Suggested Listening Level: Grades 6–8

The Wolves of Willoughby Chase BY JOAN AIKEN. *Illustrated by Pat Marriott.* New York: Doubleday & Company, 1962. Paperback: Dell, 1981.

The author claims this novel is set in a history that never was, within reach but turned upside down with the Stuarts on the throne of England instead of Queen Victoria. One doesn't have to be a history buff to follow this melodrama, however, for the plethora of detail and strong sense of characterization catch both reader and listener from the very first wolf-howl.

Arriving at Willoughby Chase in a swirling snowstorm, the ominous Miss Slighcarp ("a tall, thin lady clad from neck to toe in a traveling dress of swathed gray twill") is only the first of several threats to Bonnie, dark and impetuous, and her cousin, the fair, sweet, and loyal Sylvia. Miss Slighcarp is joined by Josiah Grimshaw, and when Bonnie's father is called away on an extended trip, the two villains banish our heroines to a dreadful charity school where misdeeds are punished by isolation in the coal cellar. Clever Bonnie is aided by a vagabond named Simon, however, and the three children escape from the charity school to find safety with poor Aunt Jane, who needs their help as much as they need her. Before the final curtain falls, parents return, the villains are punished, and wolf-howls fade into soft, warm dreams.

Rich, vivid detail and exciting "cliff-hanging" episodes make this and its sequels experiences middle-grade listeners should not miss. The ten chapters of this novel require about twenty-five to thirty minutes' reading time each.

Suggested Listening Level: Grades 4–6

The Wonderful Flight to the Mushroom Planet   BY ELEANOR CAMERON. *Illustrated by Robert Henneberger.* Boston: Atlantic–Little, Brown, 1954.

" 'Great jumping kadiddle fish!' shouted Chuck. 'You must invent all *sorts* of miraculous things, Mr. Bass.' " Chuck and David have brought their homemade spaceship to Mr. Tyco M. Bass's house at 5 Thallo Street. They are answering a green-inked newspaper notice looking for a boy and a spaceship and promising adventure and "a chance to do a good deed." Although an inventor of marvelous contraptions, Mr. Bass needs their help to save his ancestral planet, Basidium, where there has been a loss of a special food that keeps the inhabitants healthy.

A remarkable blend of fantasy and speculative science, Cameron's saga of the Mushroom Planet has survived nearly thirty years. The story is lively, and even audiences born after moonwalks will be fascinated by the view of the earth from the homemade spaceship. The first two parts are each about an hour-and-a-half's reading time, with chapters grouping comfortably into twenty-minute sessions. The third part is much shorter and may be read in one long, thirty-minute session.

There are five other titles in the Mushroom Planet series.

Suggested Listening Level: Grades 2–5

Zlateh the Goat and Other Stories BY ISAAC BASHEVIS SINGER. Translated from the Yiddish by the author and Elizabeth Shub. *Illustrated by Maurice Sendak.* New York: Harper & Row, 1966.

For the stories in this, Singer's first volume of stories for children, the Nobel prize–winning author draws on the rich lore of his East European Jewish childhood.

One of the most appealing of the stories is "The First Shlemiel." When Mrs. Shlemiel has to go out and leaves her husband to mind the rooster and the baby, she tells him that the jam she is saving for Hanukkah is poison, so he won't eat it up. Alas, Shlemiel falls asleep, the rooster escapes, and the baby falls out of the cradle, bumping his head. Shlemiel trembles at the thought of his wife's coming anger and decides there's no point in living such a life. But how to end it? Aha —that pot of poison . . .

Two other pieces are silly stories of Chelm, the village of fools, and there are spooky stories that feature the devil himself. The title story is a realistic tale of a boy and his beloved goat, who save each other's lives during a terrible blizzard. It and several of the other stories are set at Hanukkah time and might be shared as part of holiday festivities. In the years since this book was published, Singer has written many more good stories for children, including *Day of Pleasure*, an autobiographical account of growing up in Warsaw.

Suggested Listening Level: Grades 1–8

V/Narrowing It Down:

CROSS-LISTINGS OF THE RECOMMENDED BOOKS BY SUBJECT, LENGTH, AND TYPE

When you need to choose one book, knowing 140 good ones is hardly better than knowing none. To help you choose the best book for particular children at a particular time, we have drawn up a cross-listing of the recommended titles according to the categories that, in our experience, people most often specify when searching for children's books. The suggested listening level following each annotation will help also in locating the right book, of course.

Since some of the best books on our list don't fit neatly into any category, we hope you will use these cross-listings only as a rough guide for specific needs or interests and will also browse through the main annotated list in Chapter IV for books that look appealing.

SUREFIRE—easy-to-follow stories of universal appeal; good for inexperienced listeners and/or readers

By the Great Horn Spoon!
Charlotte's Web
The Cricket in Times Square
Fantastic Mr. Fox

The Great Brain
How to Eat Fried Worms
Mr. Popper's Penguins
Mrs. Frisby and the Rats of NIMH
Owls in the Family
Ozma of Oz
Ramona the Pest
A Toad for Tuesday
The Wonderful Flight to the Mushroom Planet

WIDE AGE-RANGE—recommended for reading to children widely spaced in age; good for family reading

Abel's Island
About Wise Men and Simpletons
The Adventures of Tom Sawyer
The Animal Family
By the Great Horn Spoon!
Charlotte's Web
Cheaper by the Dozen
The Chronicles of Robin Hood
The Complete Peterkin Papers
The Dollhouse Caper
Fantastic Mr. Fox
The Great Brain
The Hobbit
The House of Wings
How to Eat Fried Worms
The Incredible Journey
Just So Stories
The Knee-High Man
The Lemming Condition

The Lion, the Witch and the Wardrobe
Many Moons
The Mousewife
Owls in the Family
The Piemakers
Ramona the Pest
The Rescuers
Rootabaga Stories
Tatterhood and Other Tales
Thistle and Thyme
Tuck Everlasting
The Wind in the Willows
Zlateh the Goat and Other Tales

For YOUNGER LISTENERS—good choices for children of second grade and younger (see annotation for specific level suggested)

About Wise Men and Simpletons
All-of-a-Kind Family
And Then What Happened, Paul Revere?
A Bear Called Paddington
Ben and Me
Charlotte's Web
Child of the Silent Night
The Courage of Sarah Noble
The Cricket in Times Square
Fanny's Sister
Fantastic Mr. Fox
The Great Brain
The Iron Giant
Little House in the Big Woods

Many Moons
Mary Poppins
The Mousewife
Mr. Popper's Penguins
My Father's Dragon
Ozma of Oz
Ramona the Pest
Striped Ice Cream
Tatterhood and Other Tales
Thistle and Thyme
A Toad for Tuesday
The Wheel on the School
The Wind in the Willows
Winnie-the-Pooh
The Wonderful Flight to the Mushroom Planet
Zlateh the Goat and Other Tales

ONE-SESSION READS—stories short enough to be completed in one sitting; some of these volumes contain one story, and others are collections of one-session stories

About Wise Men and Simpletons
And Then What Happened, Paul Revere?
The Complete Peterkin Papers
The Cow-Tail Switch and Other West African Stories
Fanny's Sister
The Golden Treasury of Myths and Legends (some selections)
Hans Andersen: His Classic Fairy Tales
The Hundred Penny Box

Just So Stories
The Knee-High Man
Many Moons
Mouse Woman and the Vanished Princesses
The Mousewife
Oliver Hyde's Dishcloth Concert
The Other World
Rootabaga Stories
The Shrinking of Treehorn
Tatterhood and Other Tales
Thistle and Thyme
Wild Animals, Gentle Women

SHORTER STORIES—books that can be read in two hours or less but are longer than one-session reads

Abel's Island
The Animal Family
Burnish Me Bright
The Courage of Sarah Noble
The Dollhouse Caper
Fantastic Mr. Fox
Fog Magic
The Golden Treasury of Myths and Legends
   (some selections)
The Gull s Way
The Iron Giant
The Lemming Condition
The Light Princess
Mister Corbett's Ghost
Owls in the Family
Portrait of Ivan

Soup
Striped Ice Cream
A Toad for Tuesday
The White Archer

LONGER READS—stories that spin out over many reading sessions

The Adventures of Tom Sawyer
. . . and Now Miguel
Bert Breen's Barn
The Chronicles of Robin Hood
Hobberdy Dick
The Hobbit
M.C. Higgins, the Great
Red Fox
The Secret Garden
Treasure Island
Watership Down
The Wind in the Willows
The Wizard of Earthsea

Books with SEQUELS—stories that are continued for more than one volume

The Adventures of Tom Sawyer
The Alfred Summer
Alice's Adventures in Wonderland
All-of-a-Kind Family
Anastasia Again!
A Bear Called Paddington
The Borrowers
The Bully of Barkham Street

Burnish Me Bright
Cheaper by the Dozen
The Cricket in Times Square
Five Children and It
From Anna
The Good Master
The Great Brain
Henry Reed, Inc.
The House with a Clock in Its Walls
The Lion, the Witch and the Wardrobe
Little House in the Big Woods
Mary Poppins
Misty of Chincoteague
The Moffats
My Father's Dragon
Over Sea, Under Stone
Ozma of Oz
Ramona the Pest
The Rescuers
Roll of Thunder, Hear My Cry
Roller Skates
The Saturdays
The Shrinking of Treehorn
Soup
A Stranger at Green Knowe
A Toad for Tuesday
Where the Lilies Bloom
The White Mountains
Winnie-the-Pooh
The Wizard of Earthsea
The Wolves of Willoughby Chase
The Wonderful Flight to the Mushroom Planet

ADVENTURE—stories of action and suspense

The Adventures of Tom Sawyer
April Morning
By the Great Horn Spoon!
The Chronicles of Robin Hood
Escape from Warsaw
Fantastic Mr. Fox
The Hobbit
The Incredible Journey
Island of the Blue Dolphins
Journey Outside
Julie of the Wolves
The Mouse and His Child
Mrs. Frisby and the Rats of NIMH
Over Sea, Under Stone
Ozma of Oz
The Rescuers
The Sword and the Grail
A Toad for Tuesday
Treasure Island
Watership Down
Westmark
The Wheel on the School
The White Mountains
The Wizard of Earthsea
The Wolves of Willoughby Chase
The Wonderful Flight to the Mushroom Planet

ANIMALS—real and fanciful birds and beasts

Abel's Island
The Animal Family

A Bear Called Paddington
Ben and Me
Charlotte's Web
The Cricket in Times Square
Fantastic Mr. Fox
The Fledgling
The Gull's Way
The House of Wings
The Incredible Journey
Julie of the Wolves
Just So Stories
The Lemming Condition
The Lion, the Witch and the Wardrobe
Misty of Chincoteague
The Mouse and His Child
Mouse Woman and the Vanished Princesses
The Mousewife
Mr. Popper's Penguins
Mrs. Frisby and the Rats of NIMH
My Father's Dragon
Owls in the Family
The Peppermint Pig
Rascal
Red Fox
The Rescuers
Sounder
A Stranger at Green Knowe
A Toad for Tuesday
Watership Down
The Wheel on the School
Wild Animals, Gentle Women
The Wind in the Willows

All kinds of FAMILIES

The Alfred Summer
All-of-a-Kind Family
Anastasia Again!
. . . and Now Miguel
The Animal Family
Aunt America
The Borrowers
The Bully of Barkham Street
Calico Bush
Cheaper by the Dozen
Childtimes
The Complete Peterkin Papers
The Courage of Sarah Noble
The Dollhouse Caper
Dragonwings
The Endless Steppe
Escape from Warsaw
A Fair Wind for Troy
Fanny's Sister
Five Children and It
The Good Master
The Great Brain
The Hundred Penny Box
Little House in the Big Woods
M. C. Higgins, the Great
Mrs. Frisby and the Rats of NIMH
The Moffats
The Mouse and His Child
The Peppermint Pig
Portrait of Ivan

Ramona the Pest
Rascal
Roll of Thunder, Hear My Cry
Roosevelt Grady
The Saturdays
The Shrinking of Treehorn
Sounder
Striped Ice Cream
Where the Lilies Bloom

FOLKLORE—folk and fairy tales, myth and legend

About Wise Men and Simpletons
American Tall Tales
The Chronicles of Robin Hood
The Cow-tail Switch and Other West African
   Stories
A Fair Wind for Troy
The Golden Treasury of Myths and Legends
The Knee-high Man
Mouse Woman and the Vanished Princesses
The Other World
The Sword and the Grail
Tatterhood and Other Tales
Thistle and Thyme
The White Archer
Zlateh the Goat and Other Stories

HISTORICAL PERSPECTIVES—books that illumine the past

Across Five Aprils
The Adventures of Tom Sawyer
All-of-a-Kind Family

. . . and Now Miguel
And Then What Happened, Paul Revere?
April Morning
Ben and Me
Bert Breen's Barn
By the Great Horn Spoon!
Calico Bush
Children of the Fox
The Chronicles of Robin Hood
The Courage of Sarah Noble
Dragonwings
The Endless Steppe
Escape from Warsaw
A Fair Wind for Troy
The Good Master
Harriet Tubman, Conductor on the Underground Railroad
Hobberdy Dick
Little House in the Big Woods
Orphans of the Wind
Roll of Thunder, Hear My Cry
Sounder
The Witch of Blackbird Pond

HUMOR—witty books, funny books

Alice's Adventures in Wonderland
American Tall Tales
Anastasia Again!
A Bear Called Paddington
Ben and Me

By the Great Horn Spoon!
Cheaper by the Dozen
The Complete Peterkin Papers
The Ears of Louis
Fantastic Mr. Fox
Five Children and It
The Great Brain
Henry Reed, Inc.
How to Eat Fried Worms
The Light Princess
Many Moons
The Moffats
Mr. Popper's Penguins
My Father's Dragon
Owls in the Family
The Piemakers
The Phantom Tollbooth
The Pushcart War
Ramona the Pest
The Shrinking of Treehorn
Soup
Winnie-the-Pooh
(See also individual tales in the folklore collections)

MYSTERIES—books that keep you guessing

The Dollhouse Caper
The Egypt Game
Fog Magic
From the Mixed-up Files of Mrs. Basil E.
   Frankweiler

The House with a Clock in Its Walls
Journey Outside
Mister Corbett's Ghost
Moon Eyes
The Return of the Twelves
A Stranger Came Ashore
Tom's Midnight Garden
Westmark

NONFICTION—accounts of real lives, animal and human

And Then What Happened, Paul Revere?
Child of the Silent Night
Childtimes
The Endless Steppe
Flying to the Moon
The Gull's Way
Harriet Tubman, Conductor on the Underground
   Railroad
Rascal
Wild Animals, Gentle Women

OTHER WORLDS—imaginary realms of one sort or another

Alice's Adventures in Wonderland
The Animal Family
The Borrowers
Fog Magic
The Hobbit
Journey Outside
The Mouse and His Child

Mouse Woman and the Vanished Princesses
My Father's Dragon
The Other World
The Phantom Tollbooth
Tom's Midnight Garden
The White Mountains
The Wizard of Earthsea

STRANGE CREATURES—tales of ghosts, giants, goblins, and such

Alice's Adventures in Wonderland
American Tall Tales
The Animal Family
The Golden Treasury of Myths and Legends
Hobberdy Dick
The Hobbit
The House with a Clock in Its Walls
The Iron Giant
The Lion, the Witch and the Wardrobe
Mister Corbett's Ghost
Moon Eyes
Mouse Woman and the Vanished Princesses
My Father's Dragon
The Other World
Ozma of Oz
The Phantom Tollbooth
A Stranger Came Ashore
The Sword and the Grail
The White Mountains
The Wizard of Earthsea
The Wonderful Flight to the Mushroom Planet

SURVIVAL STORIES—Crusoe's descendants

Abel's Island
Escape from Warsaw
The Endless Steppe
Fantastic Mr. Fox
The Incredible Journey
Island of the Blue Dolphins
Journey Outside
Julie of the Wolves
Mrs. Frisby and the Rats of NIMH
Slake's Limbo
A Toad for Tuesday
Treasure Island
Watership Down

VI/Book-Places:

FOR TRAVELERS AND STAY-AT-HOMES, A CROSS-LISTING OF BOOKS BY SETTINGS

This chapter lists books in which a specific setting plays a prominent part and arranges them by location, so that readers interested in a particular city, region, or country can locate books that depict that area. Just as a young child's familiarity with the classic picture book *Make Way for Ducklings* adds to the delight of a swanboat ride in Boston's Public Gardens, so a reading of *. . . and Now Miguel* will add a rich dimension to a family's stay in New Mexico. And books can deepen the understanding and appreciation of our everyday surroundings as well. New York City dwellers learn from *Roller Skates* what their city was like to a ten-year-old in the 1890s—and discover in *The Pushcart War* what it may be like in years to come if the traffic gets any worse!

UNITED STATES AND CANADA

> *Calico Bush:* coast of Maine
> *The Gull's Way:* coast of Maine
> *And Then What Happened, Paul Revere?:* Boston, Massachusetts
> *April Morning:* Lexington, Massachusetts

The Fledgling: Concord, Massachusetts
The Witch of Blackbird Pond: Connecticut
The Courage of Sarah Noble: Connecticut
Bert Breen's Barn: upstate New York
All-of-a-Kind Family: New York City
The Cricket in Times Square: New York City
*From the Mixed-Up Files of Mrs. Basil E. Frank-
   weiler:* New York City
The Pushcart War: New York City
Roller Skates: New York City
The Saturdays: New York City
Slake's Limbo: New York City
Ben and Me: Philadelphia
*Harriet Tubman, Conductor on the Underground
   Railroad:* Tidewater, Maryland
Misty of Chincoteague: coast of Virginia
Childtimes: North Carolina; Washington, D.C.
Where the Lilies Bloom: Great Smoky Mountains,
   North Carolina
Orphans of the Wind: coast of South Carolina;
   Virginia (also Bristol, England)
Queenie Peavy: Georgia
Sounder: southern United States
Portrait of Ivan: Florida
Roll of Thunder, Hear My Cry: Mississippi
Rootabaga Stories: midwestern United States
Across Five Aprils: southern Illinois
The Adventures of Tom Sawyer: Hannibal, Mis-
   souri
Little House in the Big Woods: Wisconsin (se-
   quels: Kansas, Minnesota, South Dakota)
Rascal: Wisconsin

The Loner: Montana
The Great Brain: Utah
. . . and Now Miguel: northern New Mexico
The Egypt Game: California
By the Great Horn Spoon!: San Francisco, California
Dragonwings: San Francisco, California
Mouse Woman and the Vanished Princesses: Pacific coast, northwest United States and southwest Canada
Julie of the Wolves: Alaska
The White Archer: Canadian Arctic
Owls in the Family: Ontario
The Incredible Journey: northwest Ontario

Red Fox: New Brunswick
Fog Magic: Nova Scotia

GREAT BRITAIN

A Bear Called Paddington: London
Mary Poppins: London
Mister Corbett's Ghost: London
Watership Down: Hampshire
Over Sea, Under Stone: Cornwall
Hobberdy Dick: the Cotswolds
A Stranger at Green Knowe: the Midlands (also the Belgian Congo)
Tom's Midnight Garden: East Anglia
The Peppermint Pig: Norfolk
The Chronicles of Robin Hood: Sherwood Forest (Nottinghamshire)
The Return of the Twelves: Yorkshire
The Secret Garden: Yorkshire
Thistle and Thyme: Scotland
A Stranger Came Ashore: Shetland Islands
The Other World: Celtic Britain, Brittany

CONTINENTAL EUROPE

The Wheel on the School: Holland
Burnish Me Bright: France
Shadow of a Bull: Spain
The Good Master: Hungary
Zlateh the Goat and Other Tales: Poland
Escape from Warsaw: Warsaw, Poland, and Germany
Children of the Fox: Greece

A *Fair Wind for Troy:* Greece
Aunt America: Ukraine, Soviet Union
The Endless Steppe: Siberia (also Vilna, Poland)

AFRICA

The Cow-tail Switch and Other West African Stories: West Africa

AUSTRALIA

A Racecourse for Andy: Sydney

Appendix A: Poetry

Any program of reading aloud should include poetry, for poetry more than any other form of literature is written to be heard. A carefully selected poem, presented with enthusiasm, may very well become part of a family's or a class's common experience, to be quoted with relish again and again. "And the highwayman came riding, riding, riding . . ." chanted one group of children as they left the library. They had been intrigued by comic books superheroes, Spiderman being the current favorite, and Alfred Noyes's poem turned out to be a perfect choice. A first-grade class demanded Ogden Nash's "The Tale of Custard the Dragon" over and over again and could quote whole segments.

There are so many wonderful volumes of poetry for children available—anthologies, illustrated versions of one poem, and collections of a single poet's work—that to list and annotate them all would require a volume by itself. Therefore, we have listed eight titles to represent hundreds. Brief comments indicate why we recommend them as a starting point, but we urge you to look at others that please you and your audience.

A Child's Garden of Verses by Robert Louis Stevenson. Multiple editions.

Today's children find, just as their grandparents did, that Stevenson knows all about what it's like to be a child—from the injustice of "Bed in Summer" to the sheer delight of "The Swing." His poems are available in many editions, including an inexpensive paperback selection of those poems that most appeal to younger children, illustrated by the outstanding artist Erik Blegvad (Random House, 1978).

The Golden Treasury of Poetry edited by Louis Untermeyer. Illustrated by Joan Walsh Anglund, Western Publishing Co., Golden Press, 1959.

Well-known anthologist Louis Untermeyer has compiled a collection of range and depth—from Mother Goose to William Butler Yeats; from Father William to the Pied Piper to Annabel Lee. The volume contains little recent poetry, however, so it needs to be used in conjunction with one of the other collections. This fat book would be a perfect gift for a grandmother or a new teacher.

I Am the Darker Brother: An Anthology of Modern Poems by Black Americans edited by Arnold Adoff. Macmillan, 1970.

"I too sing America," wrote Langston Hughes. This collection contains poems by Hughes, Gwendolyn Brooks, and many other distinguished poets.

One at a Time by David McCord. Illustrated by Harry B. Kane. Little, Brown, 1977.

David McCord has the ear of a master poet, the vision of a child, and the sense of a wizard. This is a selection of some of his best.

Piping Down the Valleys Wild edited by Nancy Larrick. Illustrated by Ellen Raskin. Delacorte Press, 1975.
Larrick has compiled a good basic anthology for the elementary-school-aged child that combines high literary standards with a sensitivity to children's own poetry preferences.

The Poetry Troupe: An Anthology of Poems to Read Aloud compiled and decorated by Isabel Wilner. Charles Scribner's Sons, 1977.
This excellent collection is partly based on children's selections of poems *they* like to read aloud.

Reflections on a Gift of Watermelon Pickle and Other Modern Verse compiled by Stephen Dunning, Edward Lueders, and Hugh Smith. Lothrop, Lee & Shepard, 1967.
This is an unusually attractive anthology of contemporary poetry for older listeners.

When We Were Very Young by A. A. Milne. Illustrated by Ernest H. Shepard. Dutton. 1924. Paperback: Dutton, 1966; Dell, 1975.
Nobody should grow up without meeting James James Morrison Morrison . . . or hearing the thumps and bumps on the stairs.

General Guidelines for Reading Poetry to Children

Before you begin, read a few poems to yourself so that they are not mechanical, with a forced rhythm or rhyme. (If you can substitute "de dum, de dum, de dum" for a line, your reading is forced.) Then choose some that you enjoy to try with your listeners.

For children up through six or seven, for the most part select rhyming poems with a decided rhythm. These children like humorous poems and poems that tell a story. They are less enthusiastic about descriptive poems heavily dependent on figurative language. Older children, too, like humorous and narrative poetry, rhythm, and rhyme, but they also respond to free verse, to lyric poetry, to serious subjects, and to more abstract imagery and figurative language.

Don't restrict yourself either to the classic poets of childhood or to contemporary poets who write for children. Every child deserves to know *A Child's Garden of Verses* and the work of Edward Lear, Walter de la Mare, and A. A. Milne—poems and verses that have delighted children for generations. Her or his introduction to poetry would be incomplete, however, without also knowing the excellent work of contemporary poets who have written for children, such as David McCord, Karla Kuskin, Nikki Giovanni, X. J. Kennedy, and Myra Cohn Livingston.

Don't overlook poems that were not written with children in mind as readers but are simple enough for them to appreciate. Children respond enthusiastically to the poetry of William Blake, Robert Frost, Langston Hughes, Emily Dickinson, and Theodore Roethke, among others.

Finally, don't feel you have to explain the "meaning" of a poem after reading it or that the child listener should be able to do so. Children's felt response to poetry (as to other forms of literature) is far in advance of their ability to talk about it abstractly. It helps to keep in mind, too, that if the content of a poem could be expressed in prose, there would be no need to write it as a poem.

Appendix B: A Selected Bibliography

For adults who want to explore further reading aloud to children and related subjects.

Books

Butler, Dorothy. *Babies Need Books*. Atheneum, 1980. Sound advice on sharing books with children from infancy through the age of five.

Chambers, Aidan. *Introducing Books to Children*. Heinemann, 1973. (Available in the United States through *The Horn Book*.) A comprehensive and thoughtful exploration by a first-rate critic and teacher.

Cook, Elizabeth. *The Ordinary and the Fabulous*. Second edition. Cambridge University Press, 1976. "An introduction to myths, legends, and fairy tales for teachers and story tellers"; contains good advice on how to select the best version of a particular story.

Duff, Annis. *"Bequest of Wings": A Family's Pleasure with Books* and *"Longer Flight": A Family Grows Up with Books*. The Viking Press, 1944 and 1955.

Hearne, Betsy. *Choosing Books for Children: A Com-*

monsense Guide. Delacorte Press, 1981. An intelligent and lively resource for parents.

Larrick, Nancy. *Encourage Your Child to Read: A Parent's Primer*. Dell, 1980. An inexpensive "purse book" that covers the basics well.

————. *A Parent's Guide to Children's Reading*. Fourth edition. Doubleday, Bantam Books, 1975. This has long been a valuable asset to concerned parents.

Sartain, Harry W., ed. *Mobilizing Family Forces for Worldwide Reading Success*. International Reading Association, 1979.

Winn, Marie. *The Plug-In Drug: Television, Children and the Family*. The Viking Press, 1977. A thought-provoking indictment of television's impact on children.

Articles

Chomsky, Carol. "Stages in Language Development and Reading Exposure." *Harvard Educational Review* 42 (1972), 1–33.

Jolly, Thomas. "Would You Like for Me to Read You a Story?" *The Reading Teacher* (May 1980), 994–97. A summary of ERIC/RCS microfiche materials on reading aloud.

McCormick, Sandra. "Should You Read Aloud *To* Your Children?" *Language Arts* 54 (February 1977), 139–43, 163. Reviews research studies assessing the value of reading aloud to children.

Sharp, Wendy. "The Paperback Job." *The Horn Book* (February 1981), 91–97. A master teacher describes her techniques for enriching her students' days with literature.

Shattuck, Roger. "How to Rescue Literature." *The New York Review of Books,* April 17, 1980, 29–35. Argues that hearing literature read aloud is essential to literary study at all levels.

Singer, Dorothy G. "Reading, Imagination, and Television." *School Library Journal* 26 (December 1979), 31–34.

Smith, Frank. "Demonstrations, Engagement and Sensitivity: The Choice Between People and Programs." *Language Arts* 58 (September 1981), 634–42. Warns that technology is restricting the time available for teacher-originated activities like reading aloud.

Teale, William H. "Positive Environments for Learning to Read: What Studies of Early Readers Tell Us." *Language Arts* 55 (November/December 1978), 922–32.

Appendix C: A Personal Record of Books Read Aloud

The following pages are included to encourage parents and teachers using this book to make a record of the books they have read to children. (If you have borrowed this volume from a library, however, please do *not* write in it. An inexpensive spiral-bound notebook can serve the same purpose. Just label it "Books Read Aloud" and enter headings like those below.) Kept by a parent, such a record becomes part of the family archives. As the children grow up they will find that the titles and comments, like favorite snapshots, stimulate rich memories. We've observed that many new parents become interested in the books they knew in childhood and want to share their favorites with their own children. If a record has been kept, they'll be spared asking their local librarian "Do you know a book about a boy who gets lost in a blizzard while taking a goat to the butcher? I'm afraid I don't remember the title or author."

The record can help teachers to remember what they have read in years past and to refine their sense of what types of books are most successful with classes of a particular grade or ability level. They can use it to recommend effective books to other teachers, and to coordinate their read-aloud choices with those of others in the school, so that the same children don't hear *Charlotte's Web* in first, second, and third grade. (It has happened, we've heard.)

Finally, by adding here or in your notebook titles that do not appear on our recommended list—books that you've discovered and read aloud—you will supplement and personalize this guide, thus making it even more useful.

A PERSONAL RECORD OF BOOKS READ ALOUD

BOOK TITLE	DATE OF READING	LISTENERS	RATING AND/OR REACTIONS
Charlotte's Web	December 1982	Matthew and Sarah	Like Wilbur, we'll never forget Charlotte. We didn't want the book to end.
The Mouse and His Child	March and April 1983	4th graders—"gifted" class	Good choice. After initial objections to "toy stories" as too babyish, class grew very enthusiastic. Heavy discussion followed.
Thank You, Jackie Robinson	July '82 (while camping)	whole family	A winner. Ben has been recommending it to his friends; Annie is now trying to read it on her own.

A PERSONAL RECORD OF BOOKS READ ALOUD

BOOK TITLE	DATE OF READING	LISTENERS	RATING AND/OR REACTIONS

A PERSONAL RECORD OF BOOKS READ ALOUD

BOOK TITLE	DATE OF READING	LISTENERS	RATING AND/OR REACTIONS

Index

About the Authors

MARGARET MARY KIMMEL is on the faculty of the University of Pittsburgh School of Library and Information Science, where she teaches children's literature and storytelling.

ELIZABETH SEGEL teaches children's literature courses in the English Department of the University of Pittsburgh and serves on the Core Faculty of the Women's Studies Program there.

Both authors have published widely in the field of professional literature.